# Contents

| | |
|---|---:|
| Foreword | 9 |
| *Introduction* | 13 |
| Typical Article Layout | 14 |
| Problems You May Encounter | 16 |
| Common Types of Crime | 21 |
| Involved Persons | 24 |
| Court Hierarchy | 28 |
| Police Hierarchy | 30 |

*Articles*

| | |
|---|---:|
| 1. Re-arrest in Saitama | 34 |
| 2. Police Search Yamaguchi-gumi Headquarters | 38 |
| 3. Armed Man Escapes With Cash in Tomiura | 42 |
| 4. Fatal Robbery in Isesaki | 46 |
| 5. Mans Body Found in Toshima Mansion | 50 |
| 6. Strangled Man Found in Road | 54 |
| 7. Death by Intravenous Drip in Sendai | 58 |
| 8. Illegal Loan to Gang Boss | 62 |
| 9. Hachioji Pachinko Parlour Robbed | 66 |
| 10. Graduation of Juvenile Involved in Murder | 70 |
| 11. Mother Arrested Over Dead Child | 74 |
| 12. Gang Boss Confesses to Counterfeit Notes | 78 |
| 13. Watches and Gems Stolen in Shop Raid | 82 |
| 14. Increase in Importation Bans on Fake Goods | 86 |
| 15. Illegal Re-entry Korean Linked to Teargas Incident | 90 |

*Articles (continued)*

| | |
|---|---|
| 16. Nineteen Year Old Confesses to Murder | 96 |
| 17. Arrest of Drivers for False Statements | 100 |
| 18. Re-arrest of ¥19M Robbery Suspects | 104 |
| 19. Drunken Assault on Train | 108 |
| 20. Fatal Stabbing of Man in Aichi-Anjo | 112 |
| 21. Man Not Guilty of Professional Negligence | 116 |
| 22. Discovery of Murder Suspects Body | 120 |
| 23. Drunken Driving in Hagi City | 126 |
| 24. Missing Taxi Driver Assaulted | 130 |
| 25. Man Fled After Injuring Seven in Crash | 134 |
| 26. Fingerprint on Missing Taxi Drivers Door | 138 |
| 27. Sewer Workers Killed by Toxic Fumes | 142 |
| 28. Fatal Hit-and-Run in Setagaya Ward | 146 |
| 29. Image of Man in Gyudon Shop Robbery | 150 |

*Vocabulary Lists*

| | |
|---|---|
| English to Japanese | 156 |
| Japanese to English | 164 |

| | |
|---|---|
| Afterword | 171 |

# Foreword

Since my first visits to Japan in the early '90s, I have tried to master the reading and writing of the Japanese script. The process involves the memorisation of two phonetic scripts and several thousand Chinese characters, known as 'kanji'. In the absence of the opportunity to either live in Japan, or the chance to study the language for some years in a formal educational institute, progress is inevitably slow.

However, the advent of the Internet has made it possible to be in continuous touch with Japanese society via constantly updated articles. Most Japanese newspapers and magazines have excellent websites which are usually available without payment. A number of software packages can also be downloaded free of charge, removing the need to refer continuously to traditional dictionaries.

I have found that reading short articles on a daily basis is a more pleasurable, and therefore more effective, way of learning than trying to plough through worthier but longer pieces. The repetitive use of compounds and phrases in their proper context eventually has an effect, and useful vocabulary is learned painlessly. Japan is famous as an advanced nation with a low crime rate. Although the levels of criminality are still very low compared to other countries at an equivalent level of economic development, rates of incidence of robbery, burglary and most other crimes are increasing steadily. It seems that as Japanese society becomes more mobile, then the previous norms of behaviour required of its citizens are changing.

I started looking at items on Japanese newspaper crime because I found them much more interesting than articles about heavy industry which I was obliged to read for reasons of my work. Some of these articles deal with Japan-specific crimes, such as the activities of the violent and well-established gangs known as 'Yakuza'. The majority deal with the day's latest reports of lawbreaking from all parts of Japan, sometimes in gruesome detail.

The transition for a student going from reading conventional Japanese sentences to reading newspaper articles can be tricky: Japanese journalists are required to save space, and will therefore omit sentence parts, leaving the reader to insert that which is necessary. Although there is a vast wealth of original Japanese material available via the Internet, as far as I am aware there is nothing available to help the student of Japanese who wants to read newspaper articles dealing with crime. I offer this booklet as my contribution.

My target audience is the foreign student of Japanese, not necessarily living in Japan, who has already invested some full or part-time years of study in learning how to read. This means that the hiragana and katakana scripts hold no mysteries, and the student should be able to recognise the greater part of the Joyo Kanji (defined by the Japanese Ministry of Education in 1981 as the one thousand nine hundred and forty five characters which must be used in legal and government documents, in newspapers, magazines and by the public in general). I wish to be no more prescriptive than this.

One of the main benefits of being able to read newspaper texts is that the student is freed from the dreary round of prescribed passages. The student can instead achieve mastery of the prescribed kanji set by the daily reading of news articles which are short, simple, and above all, interesting. A virtuous circle develops where the increasing ability of the student creates a thirst for reading more articles, which in turn increases the student's population of known kanji.

The preparation of this booklet has been another step forward in my own struggle to learn to read Japanese. I will be very happy if this method helps someone else to make progress. I am sure there are many corrections and improvements to be made, and I will endeavour to address all comments which I receive.

Lyon, France
12 June 2007

# Introduction

INTRODUCTION

# Typical Article Layout

The short articles on crime which can readily be found on a daily basis in print or on the internet will typically have the following features :-

a) A short title. The date, month and year of the article.

b) An introductory paragraph summarising what is to follow, giving location, names of victims and suspects, and main features of what has taken place. Often two or three sentences will suffice, but these sentences may be surprisingly (and bafflingly) long.

c) The following couple of paragraphs will provide more details on the crime, such as citing details of injuries, appearance of the assailant, or values of goods stolen.

d) The final paragraph will frequently refer to the local police station involved, and will comment on progress made so far in the investigation, and the expected outcome.

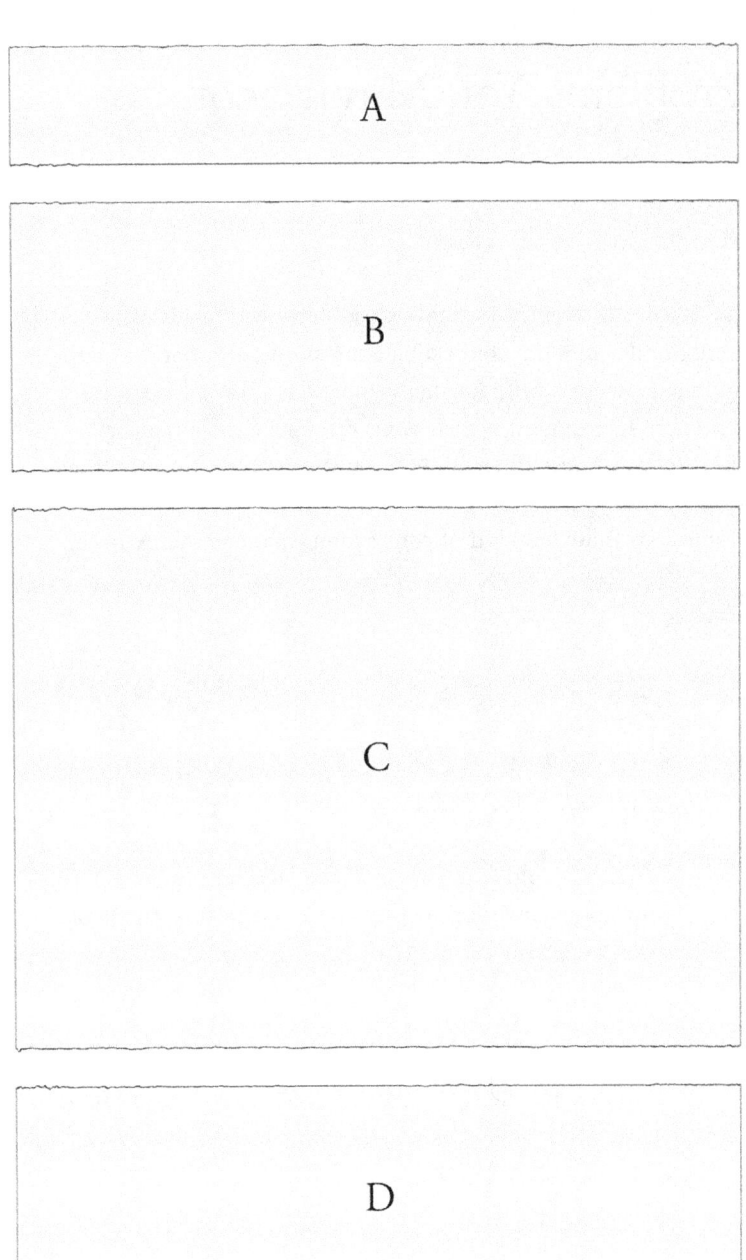

## Introduction

# Problems You May Encounter

**Missing Particles or Verbs**

For reasons of brevity, journalists use shortened forms of compounds, miss out connecting expressions, and remove particles and verbs which would normally appear in a formal Japanese sentence. The student is then obliged to make the necessary substitutions himself/herself. In the five examples shown, actual article titles from newspapers have had missing components restored to show the kind of contractions that commonly occur.

*Example 1*

広島の2歳児ひき逃げ死亡、容疑の22歳会社員逮捕。

広島の2歳児がひき逃げされて死亡した、容疑者の22歳の会社員が逮捕された。

A 22 year old company employee has been arrested for involvement in the hit-and-run death of a 2 year old boy in Hiroshima.

*Example 2*

福井の遺体切断事件、(夫の世話に疲れた)と、妻が供述。

福井県の遺体が切断された事件について、(夫の世話に疲れた)と、妻が供述した。

In the Fukui prefecture body dismemberment incident, a wife has stated that she was worn out by caring for her husband.

*Example 3*

神奈川いじめ自殺、同級生4人「不処分」。

神奈川県のいじめ自殺について、(容疑者の)同級生4人が不処分になりました。

In the suicide caused by bullying case in Kanagawa Prefecture, four fellow students will receive no punishment.

*Example 4*

１9才少年無免許運転車衝突、9人重軽傷。

19才の少年が無免許で運転していた車が衝突して、9人が重軽傷を負った。

19 year old drove without driving licence, nine people injured in crash.

*Example 5*

介護報酬不正請求、名古屋市が指定取り消しへ。

介護報酬を不正に請求したとして、名古屋市が(不正請求者を)指定取り消しへと処分しました。

The city of Nagoya has penalised dishonest seekers of care money by disallowing future claims.

## The particle 'へ'

'へ' in a headline indicates that somebody is moving towards doing something, i.e. they haven't done it yet, but are considering it or planning it.

> 大阪の送水トンネル35年ぶり全面点検へ。

> For Osaka's water supply tunnel, after a gap of 35 years, plans are being mooted for an inspection of the whole of the surface.

## Place Names

Journalists often identify exactly the location of a crime, down to the detail of which floor in which building. Place names are always a substantial hurdle for students of Japanese wishing to make certain of a translation, but happily the Internet offers a solution. The Japanese Post Office assigns a Post Code to every city, ward, town or village in Japan, and inputting a cited place-name into the Post Office Search facility will yield both the post code for the address, and more usefully, the name of the place written in katakana. Example, a cited address such as 神戸市西区伊川谷町潤和 will be tricky for most students of Japanese, but a quick search on the Post Office yields:- コウベシニシク Kobe Shinishiku for 神戸市西区 and イカワダニチョウジュンナ Ikawadanichojunna for 伊川谷町潤和.

## People's Names

Japanese family and given names pose a worse problem than place names for the student. Kanji which are not on the government list of approved Chinese characters may have been used, and readings may only be known to family and friends. For example, an acquaintance of mine has the given name 一, which can be read as ichi, kazu, moto and in other ways. None of these readings is correct: it is read 'Hashime' after the name of one elderly man in the village where he was born. Sometimes, the article will provide a reading in hiragana for an unusual name. In most cases, it is best to ask a native Japanese speaker for an informed opinion. The twenty most common Japanese family names in descending order of occurrence are:

| 漢字 | ひらがな | 英語 |
|---|---|---|
| 鈴木 | すずき | Suzuki |
| 佐藤 | さとう | Sato |
| 田中 | たなか | Tanaka |
| 山本 | やまもと | Yamamoto |
| 渡辺 | わたなべ | Watanabe |
| 高橋 | たかはし | Takahashi |
| 小林 | こばやし | Kobayashi |
| 中村 | なかむら | Nakamura |
| 伊藤 | いとう | Ito |
| 斉藤 | さいとう | Saito |
| 加藤 | かとう | Kato |
| 山田 | やまだ | Yamada |
| 吉田 | よしだ | Yoshida |
| 佐々木 | ささき | Sasaki |
| 井上 | いのうえ | Inoe |
| 木村 | きむら | Kimura |
| 松本 | まつもと | Matsumoto |
| 清水 | しみず | Shimizu |
| 林 | はやし | Hayashi |

(Source 佐久間英「日本人の姓」六芸書房(1972)佐久間ランキングより)

Any given name ending in 子 'ko' is always a female name e.g. (Yoko), and any given name ending in 二 'ji' is always a male name. E.g. 光二 (Koji).

The Post Office website mentioned above can be found at:-
https://www.post.japanpost.jp/zipcode/index.html

## INTRODUCTION

# Common Types of Crime

Below is a list of ten different types of crime often referred in Japanese crime articles.

*Arson*

大阪市で数件の不審火事件、放火罪で16才の少年が逮捕された。

In relation to the unexplained fires in Osaka City, a 16 year old boy has been arrested for arson.

*Drugs related*

「薬物犯罪への取締強化月間」で、覚せい剤の押収量が急増している事が判りました。

It is understood that the volume of stimulants seized during the monthly campaign against drug crime has sharply increased.

*Corruption*

社会保険庁の職員2名が、同庁内の収賄容疑について事情聴取を受けた。

Two staff members of National Social Security office suspected of taking bribes have been interviewed by the police.

*Murder*

現場の状況などから殺人・死体遺棄事件として、品川署に捜査本部を設置。

In the context of the murder and abandonment of a body, the Shinagawa police have set up an incident room to investigate the crime.

*Possession of Weapons Without Permission*

無職の田中博容疑者が、銃刀法違反罪で逮捕された。

Unemployed Hiroshi Tanaka has been arrested on suspicion of breaking the Swords and Firearms Control Law.

*Perjury*

弁護士の伊藤明容疑者が偽証罪で、福岡県警により逮捕された。

Lawyer Mr Akira Ito has been arrested on suspicion of perjury by Fukuoka Prefectural police.

*Forgery*

島根銀行の鈴木祥子行員が偽札五百枚の通貨偽造罪の疑いで、島根県警に取調べを受けた。

Shimane Bank employee Shoko Suzuki has been questioned by the Shimane prefectural police as a suspect in the counterfeiting of 500 yen notes.

*Patent Infringement*

厦門(アモイ)税関はこのほど、北京オリンピックマスコットの 特許権を侵害する衣類3600点を押収した。

The Amoy Customs office (in China) has confiscated 3600 items of apparel which infringe the Patent rights of the Peking Olympic Mascot.

*Illegal Entry*

横浜港で中国人八名が密入国の罪で逮捕された。

Eight Chinese nationals have been arrested in the Port of Yokohama for illegal entry into the country.

*Sexual molestation*

阪急電車内で女子高校生の下半身を触ったとして痴漢の現行 犯で逮捕されたサラリーマン。

Following the groping of a high school girl on the Hanky train line, an office worker has been arrested for sexual molestation.

# INTRODUCTION

# Involved Persons

Below is a list of ten commonly cited roles referred to in Japanese crime articles. In Japanese police procedure, it is normal practice for the investigating police officer to warn someone that they are considered a 'suspect' (容疑者), and to invite that person to acknowledge that he is a suspect. Assuming sufficient evidence has been collected, the local prosecutor lays charges against the suspect and arranges a court appearance. The suspect then becomes a defendant (被告者).

*Victim*

犯罪の被害者高橋玲子さんは損害賠償を求めるという。

Crime victim Reiko Takahashi is seeking compensation for damage.

*Defendant*

佐藤健二被告(29)の初公判が20日、横浜地裁でありました。

Defendant Kenji Sato made his first appearance in Yokohama District Court on the 20th.

*Suspect*

無職井上大介容疑者(39)を強盗強姦容疑で逮捕した。

Unemployed 39 year old Daisuke Inoe has been arrested on suspicion of robbery and rape.

*Police*

警察によると、中村容疑者を今年6月に別の事件で逮捕。

According to the police, Nakamura was arrested as a suspect in another crime in June of this year.

*Judge*

裁判官は、公判期日を6月25日から7月11日に変更 。

The judge changed the court hearing date from the 25th June until 11th July.

*Prosecutor*

山口地検では7人の検察官が公判を担当しています。

At Yamaguchi district court seven prosecutors were in charge of court hearings.

*Witness*

渡辺医師が大阪地裁に詐欺罪の証人として喚問されました。

Dr Watanabe was summoned as a witness in the fraud case at Osaka district court.

*Assailant*

鈴木浩二社員は、暴行事件の加害者として警察に連行された。

Company worker Mr Koji Suzuki was escorted to the police station for his role as an assailant in an assault case.

*Lawyer*

吉田恵子弁護士は無罪判決に満足だと語った。

The lawyer Keiko Yoshida said she was satisfied by the 'not guilty' decision.

*Crime Boss*

22日に逮捕された佐々木義男容疑者(49)は稲川会系暴力団組長だった。

Yoshio Sasaki, who was arrested on the 22nd, was a Yakuza boss linked to the Inagawa gang.

## Introduction
# Court Hierarchy

After the Second World War, the newly established constitution provided for an independent judicial system. The court hierarchy has four levels, with the highest authority being invested in the Supreme Court in Tokyo. The senior figure in the system is the Chief Justice, nominated by the Cabinet, holding the same rank as the Prime Minister.

The other Justices in the Supreme Court are also appointed by the Cabinet, approved by the Emperor and hold the same rank as Cabinet Ministers. The next level below has eight High courts located in eight major cities with jurisdiction over decisions taken in lower courts.

Fifty District courts are so-called 'Courts of First Instance' for serious matters (in other words, the place where a defendant is likely to make a first court appearance). An equal number of Family courts exist for issues such as matrimonial disputes, but also for dealing with juveniles in trouble with the law. This number of fifty provides one of each court for each Prefecture and four in Hokkaido. At the lowest level in the hierarchy, four hundred and eighty eight Summary Courts deal with low-value civil cases and minor criminal offences.

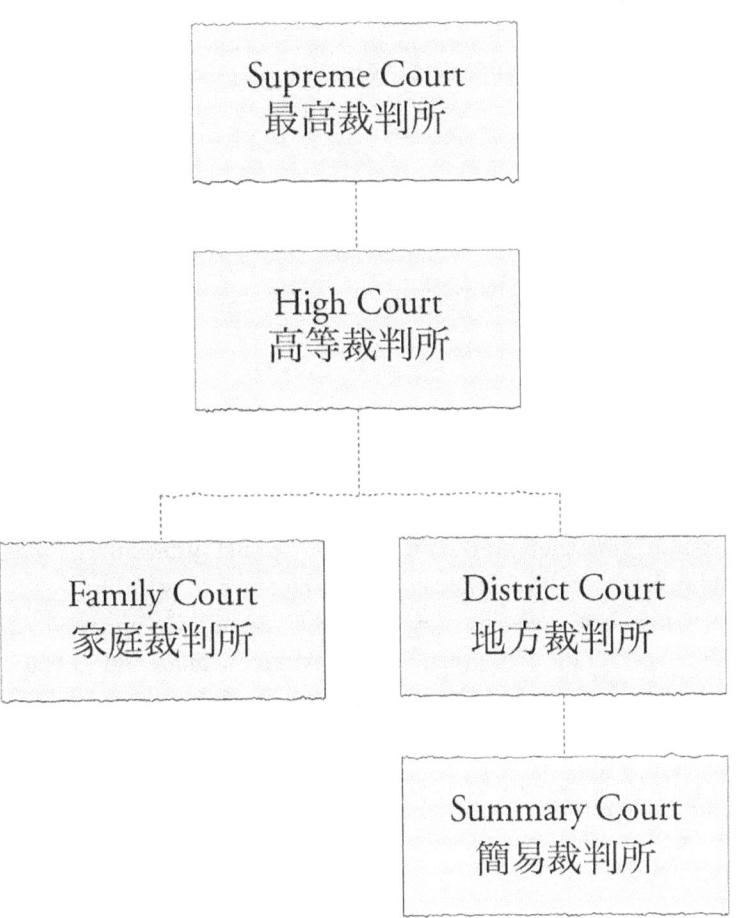

Introduction

# Police Hierarchy

There are around 280,000 police in Japan for a population of around 128 million. In common with the Court system, the national police force was established after the second world war. The well-known 'koban' police box (or 'chuzaisho' in less built-up areas) is the basis of the consensual policing system, with around 15,600 existing at local level. With a history going back to the Meiji restoration period, the Koban are open seven days a week, twenty four hours a day, and are important exchange points for all kinds of information between the police and the local population.

The koban and chuzaisho are in fact a subordinate unit of the district police stations, which in turn report to the Prefectural Police Headquarters. The Prefectural police station will be one of a number grouped under a regional police bureau, which themselves report to the National Police Agency in Tokyo. With full central control over all the police, the NPA plays a mainly administrative role, limited to establishment of budgets, training of police, statistics etc. The National Police Agency is itself controlled by the National Public Safety Commissions, under the supervision of the Cabinet Office.

# Articles

## Article 1
# Re-arrest in Saitama

2006年03月14日19時19分

1億4千万円強盗事件、主犯格の中国人を再逮埼玉

埼玉県狭山市で04年12月、ゴルフ場経営会社社長(37)宅から現金約1億4千万円などが奪われた事件で中心的な役割を果たしたとして、埼玉、石川、大阪など5府県警合同捜査本部は14日、別の強盗事件で逮捕した中国籍の住所不定、無職兪裕美(ユイ・ユイメイ)容疑者(31)強盗致傷罪などで起訴を強盗容疑で再逮捕した。兪容疑者は「そんな事件は知らない」と容疑を否認しているという。

調べでは、兪容疑者は04年12月15日早朝、実行役の中国人ら約10人と共謀し、狭山市水野の社長宅に押し入り、家族3人の手足を粘着テープで縛り、現金や高級腕時計など(1300万円相当)を奪った疑い。兪容疑者は現場には行かず、役割分担や犯行に使う車の手配など、主に指示役だったとされる。

兪容疑者を中心とする強盗団は、中国福建省出身の約15人で構成。大阪市内に拠点を置き、大阪、神奈川などで、資産家の家を狙い、二十数件の緊縛強盗を重ねたという。

## Re-arrest in Saitama of Chinese main culprit in 140 million yen robbery.

On the 14th a combined five-prefectural police investigation H.Q. (Saitama, Ishikawa, Osaka etc.) re-arrested an unemployed registered Chinese national of no fixed abode Yu Yu-mei on suspicion of robbery. He is being prosecuted for robbery with violence, and is thought to have had a central role in the incident where around 140 million yen in cash was stolen from the home of the president of a golf business in December 2004 in Sayamashi, Saitama Prefecture. Yu-mei denies involvement in the affair, saying he knows nothing of the incident.

According to the investigation, on the 15th December 2004, Yu-mei conspired with around ten other Chinese who made a forced entry into the president's house in Mizuno, Sayamashi, bound three family members hand-and-foot with adhesive tape, and stole cash and high quality wrist watches (thought to be around worth 13M yen).

Yu-mei himself did not go to the scene, his role was mainly that of giving instructions, arrangements for the car used in the crime and distribution of roles. The gang of robbers in which Yu-mei had a central position consists of around 15 people from Fuken prefecture in China. They have a base in Osaka City, and target the homes of the wealthy in Osaka, Kanagawa etc. They are believed to have amassed around twenty incidents involving tying up and robbing.

| 英語 | 漢字 | ひらがな |
|---|---|---|
| Robbery | 強盗 | ごうとう |
| Principal Offender | 主犯格 | しゅはんかく |
| Rob, to | 奪う | うばう |
| Investigation | 捜査 | そうさ |
| Arrest | 逮捕 | たいほ |
| Suspect | 容疑 | ようぎ |
| Bind, to | 縛る | しばる |
| Bind tightly | 緊縛 | きんばく |

## Article 2
# Police Search Yamaguchi-gumi HQ

2006年03月15日18時48分

山口組総本部を家宅捜索6代目組長就任後では初

大阪府警は15日、指定暴力団山口組の総本部(神戸市灘区)を、同組最高幹部による詐欺未遂事件の関係先として家宅捜索した。昨年7月、司忍こと篠田建市受刑者(64)銃刀法違反罪(共同所持)で有罪確定が6代目組長に就任してから、総本部が家宅捜索を受けるのは初めて。

午後2時20分ごろ、府警捜査4課の捜査員と機動隊員計約280人が捜索に入った。

山口組では、篠田組長が昨年暮れに収監されるなどして組織に動揺が広がっているとされる。府警の捜索には、新体制下の組織の実態を解明する狙いもある。

## Search of headquarters premises of Yamagumiguchi gang First time after Inauguration of 6th Boss.

Following an attempted fraud by the gang leadership, on the 15th the Osaka Prefectural police carried out a search in Nadaku, Kobe of the headquarters of the Yamaguchi-gumi, a designated crime group. Note - the law introduced in 1998 known as the boryokudan taisakuh had as its objective the controlling of certain organised criminal gangs. Once 'designated', the activities of an organisation and its membership become subject to tighter control and inspection. The three largest designated crime groups are the Yamaguchigumi, the Sumiyoshikai and the Inagawakai, with a total membership thought to be around 57,000.

This was the first premises search of the headquarters after the inauguration of the sixth boss Shinoda Kenichi (64), himself a convict with a guilty verdict against him for violation of the Swords and Firearms Control Law.

At around 2.20 p.m. approximately two hundred and eighty riot police and investigators from the 4th section of the Prefectural police investigation department began the search.

The Yamaguchi-gumi has suffered widespread disruption to the organisation since the boss Shinoda was imprisoned at the end of last year. By use of this search, the aim of the prefectural police is to understand the condition of the organisation under the new regime.

2006年03月15日18時48分

山口組総本部を家宅捜索6代目組長就任後では初

大阪府警は15日、指定暴力団山口組の総本部(神戸市灘区)を、同組最高幹部による詐欺未遂事件の関係先として家宅捜索した。昨年7月、司忍こと篠田建市受刑者(64)銃刀法違反罪(共同所持)で有罪確定が6代目組長に就任してから、総本部が家宅捜索を受けるのは初めて。

午後2時20分ごろ、府警捜査4課の捜査員と機動隊員計約280人が捜索に入った。

山口組では、篠田組長が昨年暮れに収監されるなどして組織に動揺が広がっているとされる。府警の捜索には、新体制下の組織の実態を解明する狙いもある。

Search of headquarters premises of Yamagumiguchi gang First time after Inauguration of 6th Boss.

Following an attempted fraud by the gang leadership, on the 15th the Osaka Prefectural police carried out a search in Nadaku, Kobe of the headquarters of the Yamaguchi-gumi, a designated crime group. Note - the law introduced in 1998 known as the boryokudan taisakuh had as its objective the controlling of certain organised criminal gangs. Once 'designated', the activities of an organisation and its membership become subject to tighter control and inspection. The three largest designated crime groups are the Yamaguchigumi, the Sumiyoshikai and the Inagawakai, with a total membership thought to be around 57,000.

This was the first premises search of the headquarters after the inauguration of the sixth boss Shinoda Kenichi (64), himself a convict with a guilty verdict against him for violation of the Swords and Firearms Control Law.

At around 2.20 p.m. approximately two hundred and eighty riot police and investigators from the 4th section of the Prefectural police investigation department began the search.

The Yamaguchi-gumi has suffered widespread disruption to the organisation since the boss Shinoda was imprisoned at the end of last year. By use of this search, the aim of the prefectural police is to understand the condition of the organisation under the new regime.

| 英語 | 漢字 | ひらがな |
|---|---|---|
| Investigation | 捜索 | そうさく |
| Boss (Yakuza) | 組長 | くみちょう |
| Violent Gang | 暴力団 | ぼうりょくだん |
| Yamaguchi-gumi | 山口組 | やまぐちぐみ |
| Fraud | 詐欺 | さぎ |
| Punishment | 受刑 | じゅけい |
| Violation | 違反 | いはん |
| Guilty | 有罪 | ゆうざい |
| Imprisonment | 収監 | しゅうかん |
| Disturbance | 動揺 | どうよう |

Article 3
# Armed Man Escapes With Cash in Tomiura

2006年03月17日15時24分

信用金庫に刃物男、75万円奪い逃走千葉・富浦

17日午前11時50分ごろ、千葉県富浦町原岡の館山信用金庫富浦支店から「強盗に入られた」と110番通報があった。館山署によると、男が同支店に客を装って押し入り、「金を出せ」と包丁のようなもので脅迫。行員が差し出した現金約75万円を奪って逃げたという。同署が強盗事件として捜査している。調べでは、行員や客にけがはなかった。男は30歳ぐらいで、身長約160センチ。サングラスに上下黒っぽいフード付きジャンパー姿で、外に止めていたバイクに乗って逃走したという。

Man with knife in Shinkin Bank, flees with stolen 750,000 yen Tomiura, Chiba Prefecture.

A '110' alarm call from a branch office of the Tateyama Shinkin Bank in the Haraoka district of Tomiura in Chiba Prefecture announced a robber had gained entry at around 11.50 on the morning of the 17th. According to the Tateyama police, a man had gained access to the branch in the guise of a customer, and had made threats with an edged tool while demanding money. He escaped with around 750,000 yen in cash handed over by a bank clerk. The police are investigating the incident as a robbery.

According to the investigation, neither bank employees nor customers were injured. The man was around thirty years old, and about 160cm in height. In a hooded top, of darkish overall appearance and wearing sunglasses, he escaped by riding off on a motorbike left outside.

| 英語 | 漢字 | ひらがな |
|---|---|---|
| Shinkin Bank | 信用金庫 | しんようきんこ |
| Edged Tool | 刃物 | はもの |
| Escape | 逃走 | とうそう |
| Under pretence | 装って | よそおって |
| Kitchen knife | 包丁 | ほうちょう |
| Threaten | 脅迫 | きょうはく |

## Article 4
# Fatal Robbery in Isesaki

2006年03月18日18時10分

群馬・伊勢崎の強盗殺人事件、容疑の派遣社員ら2人逮捕

群馬県伊勢崎市の駐車場で17日夜、埼玉県熊谷市妻沼、人材派遣会社員茂木克久さん(28)が、車の中で首に刃物が刺さった状態で死んでいるのが見つかった事件で、群馬県警捜査1課と境署は18日、伊勢崎市境萩原、派遣社員利根川勝(38)と同市境中島、無職小田勝(41)の両容疑者を強盗殺人容疑で逮捕した。容疑をおおむね認めているという。

調べでは、利根川容疑者らは17日午前11時ごろ、同市境上矢島の同市境クリーンセンター駐車場で、茂木さんの首を包丁のようなもので切りつけて殺害し、現金70万~80万円を奪った疑い。茂木さんは、派遣社員二十数人分の給料を派遣先の会社に届ける途中だった。利根川容疑者と小田容疑者は派遣先の職場の知り合いで、小田容疑者は今年2月下旬まで茂木さんが勤める会社に派遣社員として登録していたという。

Fatal robbery in Isesaki, Gunma Arrest of two agency employees as suspects.

On the evening of the 17th in a car park in Isesaki, Gunma, personnel agency employee Mr Mogi Katsuhisa from Menuma, Kumagaya in Saitama was discovered dead in a car with a stab wound to the throat.

On the 18th the Sakai police and the 1st section of the Gunma criminal investigation unit arrested on charges of murder and robbery suspects Masaru Oda (41), unemployed, and Masaru Tonegawa, a temp agency worker, both of the Sakainakajima and Sakaihagiwara districts of Isesaki respectively. It is said that for the most part they have accepted their guilt.

According to the investigation, Tonegawa and his companion murdered Mr Katsuhisa by cutting his throat with a kitchen knife or similar instrument in the Sakai Clean Centre car park in Sakaikamiyajima, in Isesaki at around 11 am on the 17th, and stole 700-800,000 yen in cash. Mr Katsuhisa was doing his rounds by delivering the agency company's wages to around 20 employees.

The suspects Tonegawa and Oda had become acquainted at a place of work to which they had been sent, Oda having been registered until the end of February of this year as an agency employee in the company where Mr Katsuhisa was employed.

| 英語 | 漢字 | ひらがな |
|---|---|---|
| Murder | 殺人 | さつじん |
| Stab, to | 刺す | さす |
| Die, to | 死ぬ | しぬ |
| Police | 警 | けい |
| Investigation | 調べ | しらべ |
| Cut, to | 切る | きる |
| Killing | 殺害 | さつがい |
| Wages | 給料 | きゅうりょう |

Article 5
# Mans Body Found in Toshima Mansion

2006年03月20日22時13分

東京・豊島のマンションに男性の遺体 強盗殺人で捜査

東京都豊島区南長崎2丁目で17日未明、マンション4階の一室が焼ける火事があり、この部屋に住む情報サービス業内田超(まさる)さん(41)の遺体が見つかった。警視庁は当初は自殺とみていたが、現場の状況や死因などから、殺害後に部屋が放火されたと断定。２０日午後、目白署に捜査本部を設置し、強盗殺人などの疑いで捜査を始めた。調べでは、内田さんは服を着た状態で水を張った浴槽に仰向けに沈んでおり、中に包丁が落ちていた。手首や腹などには「ためらい傷」とみられる切り傷があり、玄関は施錠されていた。その後、(1)頭や顔、背中に殴られたような傷があり、司法解剖の結果、脳挫傷が致命傷とみられる(2)室内の複数個所が放火されている(3)外国製腕時計など所持品がなくなっているなどが判明。捜査本部はだれかが殺害し、放火した後に合鍵で施錠して逃走したとみている。内田さんは16日午後9時過ぎに知人男性と携帯電話で話したことが確認されていた。この日午後7時から10時半ごろにかけ、内田さん方で断続的に床を踏みつけるような音がするのを住民が聞いていることから、出火直前に殺害されたとみられる。

## Mans body in Mansion building in Tokyo's Toshima Investigation into fatal robbery.

Following the outbreak of fire in the one-room fourth floor apartment in which he was living in the early morning of the 17th at Minami Nagasaki 2-chome in Tokyo's Toshima ward, the body of Information Service business employee Masaru Uchida (41) has been discovered. The Metropolitan police at first regarded the matter as suicide, but because of the conditions at the scene and the cause of death, they have now decided that the room was set on fire after the murder. On the afternoon of the 20th, they established an Incident room in Mejiro police station, and started the search for culprits suspected of robbery and murder.

According to the investigation, Mr Uchida was in a clothed condition, immersed face-up in a bath filled with water, into which a knife had been dropped. Gashes and 'hesitation wounds' were thought to be on the belly and wrists, and the genkan had been locked.

After this, it was established that (1) there were wounds on his head, face and back. From the legally required autopsy, it appeared that the fatal wound was cerebral bruising, (2) at multiple places in the room fires had been lit, and (3) personal belongings such as foreign watches were missing.

| 英語 | 漢字 | ひらがな |
|---|---|---|
| Corpse | 遺体 | いたい |
| Burn, be roasted | 焼ける | やける |
| Fire | 火事 | かじ |
| Police headquarters | 警視庁 | けいしちょう |
| Suicide | 自殺 | じさつ |
| Cause of death | 死因 | しいん |
| Strike, to | 沈む | しずむ |
| Faltering wound | ためらい傷 | ためらいきず |
| Legally ordered autopsy | 司法解剖 | しほうかいぼう |
| Cerebral contusion | 脳挫傷 | のうざしょう |
| Fatal wound | 致命傷 | ちめいしょう |
| Missing, be | 無くなる | なくなる |
| Duplicate key | 合鍵 | あいかぎ |

# Article 6
# Strangled Man Found in the Road

2006年3月20日21時53分

**殺人事件:路上遺体は絞殺と判明千葉・旭署**

千葉県旭市の路上で男性の遺体が見つかった事件で、死因は首を絞められたことによる窒息死だったことが20日、分かった。県警捜査1課と旭署は同日、殺人事件と断定し捜査本部を設置した。調べでは、男性は同県銚子市の美容師、高橋慎治さん(41)で、遺体は18日午前9時半ごろ、旭市鏑木の市道脇で見つかった。死後数週間経過とみられる。関係者によると、高橋さんは1人暮らしで、自宅で美容院を経営。2月下旬に別居している母(65)に「友人と数人で出かける」と電話したのを最後に連絡が取れなくなっていた。

Murder : Confirmation that body in the street had suffered death by strangulation - Asahi Police, Chiba.

In the incident where a male body was found in the road in Asahi, Chiba, on the 20th it was learned that the cause of death was death by asphyxiation due to strangulation.

The Asahi police station and the No. 1 section of Prefectural police criminal investigation department have concluded this to be a murder case and have set up an incident room. According to the investigation, the deceased was Mr Shinji Takahashi (41), a beautician in Choshi City, and his body was discovered at around 9.30 in the morning of the 18th beside a municipal road in Kaburaki, Asahi City.

It seems some weeks had elapsed since his death. According to those concerned, Mr. Takahashi lived alone, and ran a beauty parlour at his home. At the end of February he had phoned his sixty-five year old mother, who lived separately, to say he was going out with several friends, but since then he had not been in contact.

| 英語 | 漢字 | ひらがな |
|---|---|---|
| Strangulation | 絞殺 | こうさつ |
| Strangle, to | 絞める | しめる |
| Death by suffocation | 窒息死 | ちっそくし |

## Article 7
# Death By Intravenous Drip in Sendai

2006年3月22日(水)

守被告に2審も無期懲役点滴事件、弁護団は上告

仙台の筋弛緩(しかん)剤点滴事件で、1件の殺人と4件の殺人未遂の罪に問われた准看護師守大助被告(34)の控訴審判決公判は22日午後も被告本人が不在のまま続き、田中亮一裁判長は無期懲役とした1審仙台地裁判決を「事実誤認はない」と支持、守被告の控訴を棄却した。

弁護側は即日上告した。控訴審で弁護側は「事件はでっち上げだ」と主張したが、判決理由で田中裁判長は「筋弛緩剤を誤って点滴に混入するなどという事態が、短期間に同じ病院で5件も偶然起こるとは考えがたい」と指摘。「何者かが故意に投与したのは明らか」と事件性を認定した。(共同通信)

## Life sentence at High Court hearing of defendant Mori Defending Counsel to appeal in intravenous drip affair.

In Sendai's muscle-relaxant intravenous drip affair, at the appeal trial of the defendant Daisuke Mori (34), assistant nurse accused on four counts of attempted murder and one count of murder, on the afternoon of the 22nd the defendant himself continued to be absent. Presiding judge Ryuichi Tanaka dismissed defendant Mori's appeal, maintaining that there were no factual mistakes at the No. 1 Sendai District Court decision of a Life sentence.

The Defence launched a final appeal (to the Supreme Court) the same day. At the appeal hearing, the Defence insisted that he had been framed. Judge Tanaka, speaking of the reasons for the decision, pointed out that it was hard to think of a situation where someone would mix muscle relaxant into an intravenous drip, and where five incidents would occur by chance in the same hospital in a short period of time.

He concluded that in this case, it was clear that someone had administered the medicine on purpose.

| 英語 | 漢字 | ひらがな |
|---|---|---|
| Life sentence | 無期懲役 | むきちょうえき |
| Defence counsel | 弁護団 | べんごだん |
| Appeal, to | 上告 | じょうこく |
| Attempted murder | 殺人未遂 | さつじんみすい |
| Appeal trial | 控訴審 | こうそしん |
| Sentence (judicial) | 判決 | はんけつ |
| Trial | 公判 | こうはん |
| Frame someone, to | 捏ち上げる | でちあげる |
| Defendant | 被告 | ひこく |
| Presiding judge | 裁判長 | さいばんちょう |

# Article 8
# Illegal Loan to Gang Boss

2006年3月23日21時0分

暴力団組長に不正融資4億円、興産信金の前会長ら起訴

興産信用金庫(東京都千代田区)が暴力団組長側に4億円を不正融資した背任事件で、東京地検は23日、前会長・志津努(71)(同日付で辞任)、前理事長・石原静夫(63)(同)両容疑者と、指定暴力団住吉会系組長・津久井高光容疑者(68)ら計6人を背任罪で東京地裁に起訴した。

起訴状などによると、志津容疑者らは2001年7月、津久井容疑者が実質的に経営する都内の産業廃棄物処理会社「ケントワン」が融資を申し込んできた際、同社が事実上休眠状態で貸付金の回収が不能になると知りつつ4億円を融資し、同信金に損害を与えた。志津容疑者は1996年ごろ、津久井容疑者に週刊誌記者の取材を止めてもらったことがあったため、「融資の依頼を断れなかった」と供述しているという。

一方、同地検は23日、同容疑で逮捕されたケントワン元役員ら2人を処分保留で釈放した。近く起訴猶予処分にする方針。

Prosecution of former Kosan Shinkin Chairman and associates
Illegal 400 hundred million yen loan to gang boss.

In the case of malpractice where an illegal 400 hundred million yen loan was made by the Kosan Shinkin Bank (Chiyoda Ward, Tokyo) to a gang boss, the Tokyo District Public Prosecutor's office instituted legal proceedings for criminal malpractice against a number of suspects at Tokyo District court on the 23rd. These were six in total, including former Chairman Tsutomu Shizu, (who resigned on this date) board chairman Shizuo Ishihara (63), and Takamitsu Tsukui (68), boss of the Sumi-yoshikai, a designated violent crime group.

According to the prosecution's case, in July 2001 the metropolis based Kentowon industrial waste management company, in reality run by Tsukui, had applied for a loan. Shizu had advanced the 400 hundred million yen loan even though he knew full well that the recovery of the loan was impossible, since in fact the company was in a moribund state. He thus caused a loss to the Shinkin Bank.

Shizu testified that he had not declined the loan request, because around 1996 Tsukui had done him a favour by stopping a journalist from a weekly magazine from collecting information. On the 23rd the same Public Prosecutor's office released two former senior staff members of Kentowon who had been arrested as suspects, with their case being left on file in the event of further misdemeanours.

| 英語 | 漢字 | ひらがな |
|---|---|---|
| Dishonesty | 不正 | ふせい |
| Prosecution | 起訴 | きそ |
| Sumiyoshikai | 住吉会 | すみよしかい |
| Breach of trust | 背任罪 | はいにんざい |
| Breach of trust | 損害 | そんがい |
| Release, acquittal | 釈放 | しゃくほう |
| District public prosecution | 地検 | ちけん |
| Collection, recovery | 回収 | かいしゅう |
| Kosan Shinkin Bank | 興産信用金庫 | こうさんしんようきんこ |
| Malpractice | 背任 | はいにん |
| Leaving charge on the file | 起訴猶予 | きそゆうよ |

## Article 9
# Hachioji Pachinko Parlour Robbed

2006年03月25日18時37分

パチンコ店で2千万円強奪容疑、暴力団幹部ら6人逮捕

東京都八王子市のパチンコ店で昨年11月、男性店長(28)が監禁され、店の売上金約2300万円を奪われた事件で、警視庁は25日、東京都あきる野市秋川4丁目、指定暴力団住吉会系幹部鈴木伊織容疑者(34)ら男6人を営利目的略取や強盗傷害などの疑いで逮捕した。捜査1課の調べでは、鈴木容疑者らは昨年11月7日午前4時ごろ、八王子市元横山町2丁目の路上で、帰宅する店長を乗用車に押し込んで拉致し、店長の両手を粘着テープで縛り、殴るなどの暴行を加え、所持金約3万円などを強奪。さらに同6時半ごろ、パチンコ店に店長を連れて行き、売上金2355万円を奪った疑い。店長は暴行を受けた際、顔などに軽傷を負った。

Suspects in the plundering of 20 million yen from Pachinko parlour, arrest of six gang members including boss.

In November of last year at a Pachinko parlour in Tokyo's Hachioji City, the male manager was held prisoner while 23 million yen of sales takings were stolen. On the 25th the Metropolitan Police have arrested six men on suspicion of robbery with wounding and abduction for commercial gain. These include Iori Suzuki, boss of designated crime group Sumiyoshikai, located in Tokyo's Akiruno City Akigawa 4-chome.

According to the 1st section of the police investigation unit, at around 4 o' clock in the morning on the 7th of November last year, Suzuki and his men bundled the parlour manager into his car when he was on the way home in the street at Motoyokoyamacho 2-chome in Hachioji City. They bound both hands of the parlour boss with adhesive tape, subjected him to violent blows and then stole around 30000 yen in cash which he was carrying. Then at around 6 o' clock in the morning, they dragged the manager to his Pachinko Parlour, where they are thought to have stolen the parlour's takings of 23.55 million yen.

At the time when he was undergoing the violent assault, the manager suffered minor wounds to his face from the beating he received.

| 英語 | 漢字 | ひらがな |
| --- | --- | --- |
| Followers (suffix) |  | 一ら |
| Pillage | 強奪 | ごうだつ |
| Confinement | 監禁 | かんきん |
| Proceeds | 売上金 | うりあげきん |
| Abduction | 略取 | りゃくしゅ |
| Taking captive | 拉致 | らち |

ARTICLE 10

# Graduation of Juvenile Involved in Murder and Kidnap

2006年03月25日22時29分

園児殺害の少年、中学校が卒業証書 長崎

長崎市で03年7月に起きた園児誘拐殺害事件で、当時中学1年だった加害少年(15)に、事件まで在籍していた市内の中学校が卒業証書を授与したことが分かった。少年は03年4月にこの中学に入学し、事件で補導される同7月まで通学。長崎家裁の決定で、同9月からさいたま市の児童自立支援施設「国立武蔵野学院」に入所している。卒業証書は中学校が施設に郵送。3月下旬に県中央児童相談所職員らが出席し、施設内で開かれた授与式で少年に渡したという。少年は施設入所後、中学校には学籍がない「就学猶予」の状態になっていた。今春、義務教育を終える年齢に達するため、学籍を一時的にこの中学校に戻したうえで同校が卒業判定をし、少年の卒業を認めたという。

## Juvenile implicated in killing of maternity school pupil, Middle school has awarded graduation certificate, Nagasaki.

In Nagasaki in July 2003 there took place the maternity school kidnap and murder incident. It is understood that the middle school where the young man who carried out the attack (now 15) was enrolled as a 1st year pupil before the incident, has awarded him a graduation certificate.

The juvenile started at the middle school in April 2003, and commuted to the school until July when he was taken into custody because of this affair. Following a decision by the Nagasaki family court, from September 9th he was required to attend the Juvenile Independent Support facility (The National Musashino Institute) in Saitama City. The graduation certificate was sent by the school to the facility by mail. At the end of March, it was handed over to the young man at the awards ceremony which took place within the Institute, in the presence of the Prefectural Central Juvenile Consultation Office employees.

After the young man had started at the Institute, he was no longer registered at the middle school (since his schooling was postponed).

This spring, because he had reached the age where he would have finished compulsory education, the school had decided on a graduation award, temporarily restored his registration, and the young man was allowed to graduate.

| 英語 | 漢字 | ひらがな |
|---|---|---|
| Kidnapping | 誘拐 | ゆうかい |
| Family Court | 家裁 | かさい |

ARTICLE 11
# Mother Arrested Over Dead Child

2006年3月27日 1時08分

乳児遺体遺棄:自宅押し入れに、35歳母逮捕 北海道

生後1カ月の長男の遺体を自宅押し入れに遺棄したとして、道警函館中央署は25日、北海道北斗市七重浜5、グループホーム臨時職員、村田まり子容疑者(35)を死体遺棄容疑で逮捕した。村田容疑者は殺害したことを認める 供述をしており、容疑が固まり次第、殺人容疑で再逮捕する方針。調べでは、長男の死因は窒息死とみられる。村田容疑者は長男に袋をかぶせて殺害したと供述しているといい、動機を調べている。25日午前11時ごろ、村田容疑者が夫に「車内に長男を残して買い物をし、戻ったらいなくなっていた」と連絡したため、夫が110番通報した。同日正午ごろ、同署員と夫が自宅の押し入れで遺体を発見した。

## Abandoned body of infant: left in cupboard of home, 35 year old mother arrested, Hokkaido.

In the case of the body of the one month old son left in a cupboard of her home, on the 25th officers from Hakodate Central police station in Hokkaido arrested Mariko Murata 35 of Nanaehama 5, Hokuto City, temporary care home worker, on suspicion of abandonment of a dead body.

Murata has made a statement confessing that she has killed, and as soon as suspicions become more substantiated, the objective will be to re-arrest her on charges of murder.

According to the inquiry, the boy's cause of death seems to have been by smothering. Murata has confessed that she killed the boy by smothering him with a bag, and her motive is now being sought. At around 11a.m. on the morning of the 25th, Murata contacted her husband, saying that she had left her son in the car while shopping, but on her return the boy had disappeared. Her husband had then made a 110 call to the authorities. Around noon of that day, the police and her husband had discovered the body in a cupboard in their home.

| 英語 | 漢字 | ひらがな |
|---|---|---|
| Corpse, remains | 遺体 | いたい |
| Corpse | 死体 | したい |
| Death by suffocation | 窒息死 | ちっそくし |
| Motive | 動機 | どうき |

ARTICLE 12
# Gang Boss Confesses to Counterfeit Notes

2006年3月27日3時1分

偽1万円「6000枚作った」供述の組幹部再逮捕へ

福島県内の菓子店で旧1万円札の偽札を使ったとして、昨年12月、北海道警に逮捕された指定暴力団住吉会系組幹部、石垣裕二被告(31)(偽造通貨行使などの罪で公判中)が、警視庁捜査2課の調べに「6000枚の偽札を作った」と供述していることが分かった。うち約2000枚は実際に使用されたとみられる。捜査2課は、一昨年暮れから昨年初めにかけて全国各地に出回った偽札の大半は、石垣被告を主犯格とするグループが、稲川会や山口組など他の指定暴力団系組幹部ら に売り渡したものと断定。27日、同被告ら2人を通貨偽造容疑で再逮捕する。調べによると、所属する暴力団を抜けようとしていた石垣被告は2004年秋、生活資金を稼ぐために偽札作りを計画。同年10~12月、福島市内や東京都町田市内のアパートなどで知人の工員(22)らとともにパソコンとス キャナー、プリンターを使ってA4判の紙に旧1万円札を印刷し、カッターで裁断して偽札を作った。多い時で1日700枚を偽造し、指紋が残らないよう医療用手袋を使っていた。偽札は東京・渋谷に拠点のある稲川会三本杉一家の幹部の男(35)(偽造通貨行使の罪で服役中)ら複数の組員らに売却。さらに山口組や住吉会、稲川会などの組員らに1枚3000円程度で転売されるなどして、全国各地に一斉に出回った。石垣被告は少なくとも数百万円の利益を得ていたという。昨年1月にソウルのカジノに偽1万円札420枚が持ち込まれた事件で、偽造通貨行使の疑いで逮捕された在日韓 国人の男(48)も、稲川会三本杉一家幹部の男から偽札を受け取っていたとみられる。捜査2課は、暴力団勢力の間で石垣被告の偽札の話が口コミで急速に広がり、全国各地に出回ったとみている。

## Counterfeit 10,000 yen notes, 6000 made re-arrest expected of gang boss following confession.

Hokkaido police arrested a boss of registered violent crime organisation the Sumiyoshikai in December of last year for the use of forged old 10,000 yen notes in a cake shop in Fukushima. It is understood that the defendant Yuji Ishigaki (31), currently on trial for use of counterfeit currency, has confessed that he made six thousand false notes to the No 2 Section of the criminal investigation unit of the Metropolitan Police.

Two thousand of these notes are in circulation at the moment. Most of the forged notes appeared in all parts of the country between the end of the year before last and the start of last year. The investigation team has concluded that the notes had been sold on to other bosses of registered violent crime gangs such as the Inagawa-kai and the Yamaguchigumi, with these groups regarding the defendant Ishigaki as the lead criminal. They will re-arrest the defendant and an associate on the 27th on charges of currency counterfeiting.

The investigation team alleges that the defendant Ishigaki had wished to get away from the gang to which he belonged, and in Autumn 2004 he hatched the plan for making false notes to earn some money to live on. From October to December of that year, he acted together with a 22 year-old factory worker acquaintance at apartments in Fukushima and in Machida City, Tokyo. There they printed old 10,000-yen notes on A4 stamped paper sheets by use of a PC, scanner and printer, and then they produced the counterfeit money by cutting with a sharp bladed instrument.

They frequently forged 700 notes in one day, using medical gloves which leave no fingerprint. Some forged notes were sold to the head

| 英語 | 漢字 | ひらがな |
|---|---|---|
| False | 偽 | ぎ |
| Confession | 供述 | きょうじゅつ |
| Counterfeit money | 偽札 | にせさつ |
| Forgery | 偽造 | ぎぞう |
| Police H.Q. | 警視庁 | けいしちょう |
| Inagakawai (gang) | 稲川会 | いながわかい |
| Fingerprint | 指紋 | しもん |
| Penal servitude | 服役 | ふくえき |

(35, presently in prison for use of forged notes) and associates of the Inagawakai gang Sanbonsugi family with its base in Shibuya, Tokyo. Moreover, with the notes having been resold to members of the Sumiyoshikai, the Yamaguchigumi and the Inagawakai at a rate of 3000 yen each, they appeared simultaneously on the market in all parts of the country.

It is thought that Ishigaki must have made profits running to millions of yen at the very least. There was the incident in January last year when a 48 year old Korean national living in Japan was arrested on suspicion of using forged currency after four hundred and twenty forged 10,000 yen notes were taken into a casino in Seoul. It is thought he had received them from one of the henchmen of the boss of the Inagawakai, Kazua Sanbonsugi.

The No. 2 Section team consider that with talk of Ishigaki's forged notes spreading rapidly by word of mouth throughout each gang's sphere of influence, the notes would have materialised in every part of the country.

## Article 13
# Watches and Gems Stolen in Shop Raid

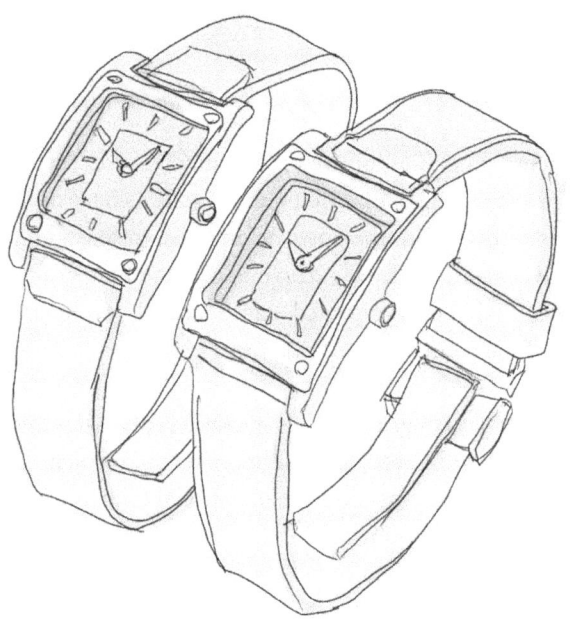

2006年3月26日11時41分

神戸のリサイクル店、時計・宝石など160点盗まれる

26日午前0時45分ごろ、神戸市西区伊川谷町潤和のリサイクル店「リサイクル市場エコ伊川谷店」で警報が鳴り、警備会社が110番通報。神戸西署員が駆けつけたところ、店舗出入り口横の窓ガラスや店内のショーケースなどが壊され、高級腕時計や財布、宝石など約160点(520万円相当)が盗まれていた。同署は窃盗事件として捜査している。調べでは、店長が帰宅した25日午後10時過ぎまでは異状はなく、窓ガラスを割るのに使ったとみられるバール(長さ約1メートル)が外に落ちていた。同署は何者かが窓から侵入したとみて調べている。

## 160 Watches, gems etc. stolen from Kobe Recycle Shop.

At 12.45 a.m. on the morning of the 26th, when the alarm sounded at the 'Recycle Market Echo Ikawadani' shop in Kobe's Nishiku Ikawadanich-junna, the security company called the emergency number 110. Officers from Kobe West police station went to the scene to find that an internal showcase and a window glass at the side of the shop's entrance way had been broken, and around 160 high quality wristwatches, wallets and gems had been stolen, with a value around 5.2 million yen.

Officers from the police station are treating the incident as a robbery. According to the investigation, there was nothing untoward until the shop manager had gone home after 10 p.m. in the evening of the 25th. A bar of around one meter length which seems to have been used to break the window glass was dropped outside. The police are investigating how someone had forced a way in through the window.

| 英語 | 漢字 | ひらがな |
|---|---|---|
| Jewels | 宝石 | ほうせき |
| Steal, to | 盗む | ぬすむ |
| Alarm | 警報 | けいほう |
| Security company | 警備会社 | けいびがいしゃ |
| Break, to | 壊す | こわす |
| Wristwatch | 腕時計 | うでどけい |
| Theft | 窃盗 | せっとう |
| Raid, intrude, to | 侵入 | しんにゅう |

Article 14
# Increase in Importation Bans on Fake Goods

2006年04月05日11時54分

偽ブランド品の輸入差し止め、中国からがトップに

昨年の偽ブランド品や特許権を侵害した商品の国内への輸入差し止め件数が、過去最高を記録したことが分かった。そのほとんどに国際郵便が使われているという。輸出国別では、中国からの件数が韓国を抜いて初めてワースト1となった。財務省関税局が4日発表した。昨年、全国9カ所の税関 が輸入を差し止めた偽ブランド品などの件数は1万3467 件。前年比47.3%の増加で、統計を取り始めた82年以降、最悪となった。

通常の税関を通らず国際郵便を使う「小口化」がここ3、4年急増しており、昨年は差し止め件数全体の96%を占めた。「港などの水際の摘発が増えたため、発覚を逃れるために国際郵便に切り替えたのでは」と同局はみている。輸出国別では、統計を取り始めた87年以降、韓国からがもっとも多かったが、昨年は中国からが半数近くの46.6%となる6278件で、初めてワースト1となった。

Banning of Importation of Counterfeit Goods, those from China top the list.

The number of cases where forged goods or products infringing patent laws have been banned from entering the country last year was at an all-time high. The International mail service has been used in most cases. Looking at these exports country-by-country, the number of incidents from China has made the country the worst case, for the first time overtaking Korea.

The Customs Department of the Finance Ministry made the announcement on the 4th. Last year, for the nine customs houses located throughout the country the number of incidents of false branded goods being prohibited entry was 13,467. This was an increase of 47.3% compared to the year before, making it the worst year since statistics were first collected in 1982. The 'small packages trend' whereby the international mail is used in bypassing the normal Customs houses has surged in the last three to four years, and last year comprised 96% of all banning incidents.

The Customs think that because there has been an increase in detection at the quayside in ports etc., there has been a switch to the international post to avoid discovery.

Looking at these exports country-by-country, from 1987 when the statistics were first compiled, most came from Korea. However, last year China became the worst offender for the first time, with 6278 incidents accounting for nearly half the incidents at 46.6% of the total.

| 英語 | 漢字 | ひらがな |
|---|---|---|
| Prohibition | 差し止め | さしとめ |
| Patent rights | 特許権 | とっきょけん |
| Infringement | 侵害 | しんがい |
| Customs office | 関税局 | かんぜいきょく |
| Exposing | 摘発 | てきはつ |

Article 15
# Illegal Re-entry Korean Linked to Teargas Incident

2006年04月07日03時01分

「強制送還後に密入国」スプレー噴射で逮捕の男が供述東京都荒川区のJR西日暮里駅であった催涙スプレー噴射事件で、警視庁が逮捕した韓国人の男が「密入国で来日した」と供述していることがわかった。男は、大阪府警に窃盗の疑いで逮捕され、昨秋、強制送還され、その直後に密入国したらしい。同庁は、男は催涙スプレーや刃物で護身してすりを繰り返す「武装すり団」の中でもより入念に武装する傾向がある釜山(プサン)出身者のグループの可能性があるとみている。傷害などの疑いで逮捕されたのは沈平根容疑者(38)。捜査3課などは、捜査資料などから、02年に大阪市内ですりをしたなどとして逮捕された韓国人と同一人物と断定した。沈容疑者は実刑判決を受けて服役後、昨年秋ごろに強制送還されたが、「昨年暮れに密入国で東京に来た」と供述しているという。同課は、送還されてすぐに来日したとみて、入国の経緯についても調べている。沈容疑者は催涙スプレーと刃渡り21センチの包丁を持っており、「護身用だった」と供述。地下鉄路線図もあったことから、同課は、逃走した3人とともに混雑する駅構内ですりの機会をうかがっていたとみている。

同課によると、催涙スプレーなどを所持してすりを繰り返す韓国人グループは02年ごろから都内で目立ち始めた。都内の韓国人武装すり団とみられる被害は、昨年は1581件で前年

より約370件増えている。ソウル出身者らでつくる「ソウルグループ」と釜山出身者らの「釜山グループ」があるとされ、04年6月には東急田園調布駅で、釜山グループの韓国人の男が包丁を振り回し、乗客らがけがをした。沈容疑者も釜山出身者という。田園調布駅の事件以降、取り締まりが強化され、すり団は一時、所持しているだけで銃刀法違反に問われる刃物は持たず、スプレーだけで護身する傾向がみられたという。しかし、今年に入ってからは釜山グループを中心に、刃物を所持したすり団の犯行が再び目立つという。今年2月、東京メトロ銀座駅ですりをしたとして同庁が逮捕した韓国人3人も、それぞれ包丁を所持し、振りかざす寸前で取り押さえたという。昨年の被害増加を受け、同課は今年1月、韓国人すりグループ掃討作戦取締本部を設置した。

Illegal entry after forced repatriation Confession of man arrested for spraying gas.

In relation to the teargas incident which took place at the Japan Rail West Nippori station in Tokyo's Arakawa Ward, it is understood that a Korean man arrested by the Metropolitan Police has confessed that he entered Japan clandestinely. Last autumn the man, arrested on suspicion of robbery by the Osaka Prefectural Police, seems to have re-entered the country clandestinely immediately after having been repatriated forcibly. The police think they can see a trend amongst the armed gangs whose men repeatedly carry out robberies whilst protecting themselves with edged tools and tear gas.

It seems to be the gangs from Pusan who are the best armed. The man arrested on suspicion of wounding is 'Chim Pyeong Geun' (38). The No 3 section of the Criminal Investigation Department has concluded from information that he was the same Korean that had been arrested for robberies in Osaka in 2002.

The suspect 'Chim Pyeong Geun', served time in prison following his courtroom appearance. He was forcibly re-patriated last year, and has confessed that he came to Tokyo as an illegal immigrant at the end of the year. The same police are investigating the circumstances around his re-entry into Japan, bearing in mind that he returned directly after being repatriated. The suspect Mr. 'Chim Pyeong Geun', who was in possession of a kitchen knife with a 21 cm blade and the tear gas, stated that these were for his own protection.

Because he was also in possession of an underground map, the police think that, together with 3 others who escaped, he was looking for pick-pocketing opportunities in the congested station premises.

According to the same police sources, Korean gangs carrying out repeated street robberies whilst armed with sprays etc. started to appear in the capital around 2002. Considering the harm done in the capital by these armed Korean pickpocket gangs, last year there were 1581 incidents, an increase of 370 cases from the year before. The 'Seoul Gang'is made up of people belonging to Seoul, and the 'Pusan Gang' formed from those from Pusan. In June of 2004 at Denenchofu station on the Tokyu Line a Korean man from the Pusan group brandished a kitchen knife and injured some passengers.

The suspect Mr 'Chim Pyeong Geun' is said to be part of the Pusan Group. After the incident at Denenchofu station, controls were strengthened, and the pick-pocket gangs ceased carrying bladed weapons, because they could be accused of infringement of the guns and swords laws for possession for a short time only. It seems there was a trend towards self-protection only by spray. However, starting this year, there has been a fresh outbreak of crimes carried out by pick-pocket gangs carrying bladed weapons, with the Pusan group being centre-stage.

In February of this year, the Police arrested three Korean men for pick pocketing at the Ginza station of the Tokyo underground system. Each was carrying a knife, and they were overwhelmed before they could draw their weapons.

| 英語 | 漢字 | ひらがな |
|---|---|---|
| Forced repatriation | 強制送還 | きょうせいそうかん |
| Tear gas | 催涙ガス | さいるいガス |
| Theft, stealing | 窃盗 | せっとう |
| Edged tool | 刃物 | はもの |
| Self-protection | 護身 | ごしん |
| Arms, armament | 武装 | ぶそう |
| Jail sentence | 実刑 | じっけい |
| Judicial decision | 判決 | はんけつ |
| Length of a sword | 刃渡り | はわたり |
| Flight, desertion | 逃走 | とうそう |
| Wield, brandish, to | 振り回 | ふりまわす |

Article 16
# Nineteen Year Old Confesses to Murder

2006年04月08日20時19分

死体遺棄容疑で19歳少年逮捕、殺害も認める供述静岡高校の同級生だった少年の遺体を畑に埋めたとして、静岡県警捜査1課と下田署は8日、同県河津町の元トラック運転手の少年(19)を死体遺棄の疑いで逮捕した。少年は殺害容疑についても認める供述をしており、県警は殺人・死体遺棄事件として捜査本部を設置し、動機などを調べている。調べでは、少年は1月26日午後9時ごろ、静岡県下田市白浜、調理師見習い藤井尊仁(たかとし)さん(19)の遺体を河津町梨本の梅畑に埋めた疑い。藤井さんは1月26日夜、外出後行方不明になり、28日に父親が捜索願を出していた。少年と藤井さんは遊び仲間。藤井さんが行方不明になる直前も少年に会っていたといい、8日朝、少年に事情を聴いたところ容疑を認め、供述通り遺体が見つかった。

## Nineteen year old juvenile arrested on suspicion of abandonment of a dead body Confession admitting murder Shizuoka.

The 1st Section of the Shizuoka Prefectural Criminal Investigation dept and the Shimoda City local police have arrested a nineteen year old former truck driver of Kawazu in Shizuoka on the 8th on suspicion of the abandonment of a body. He is thought to have buried the corpse of a school classmate in a field . The juvenile has made a statement admitting involvement in the murder. The Prefectural police have established an incident room for the murder/body concealment case and are looking into possible motives.

According to the investigators, the young man is thought to have buried the body of trainee chef Takatoshi Fujii in a plum orchard in Nashimoto in the town of Kawazu at around 9 pm on the evening of the 26th January. The deceased was from Shirahama in Shimoda City in Shizuoka.

On the evening of the 26th, the whereabouts of Fujii was unknown after he went out, and on the 28th his father asked for a search. The accused juvenile and Fujii were in the same group of mates. It can safely be said that Fujii and the accused young man met just before Fujii went missing. On the morning of the 8th when the juvenile was interviewed, he accepted his involvement, and the body was found from the statement which he made.

| 英語 | 漢字 | ひらがな |
|---|---|---|
| Abandonment | 遺棄 | いき |
| Bury, to | 埋める | うめる |
| Missing, unaccounted for | 行方不明 | ゆくえふめい |

# Article 17
# Arrest of Drivers for False Statements

2006年04月07日19時29分

裁判でうその証言をした2運転手を逮捕、福岡地検

福岡地検特別刑事部は7日、交通事故をめぐる公判でうその証言をしたとして、福岡県新宮町湊、会社員伊藤宏(35)、同県粕屋町内橋、会社員長谷部 勝利(34)の2容疑者を偽証などの疑いで逮捕した、と発表した。偽証をもとに福岡地裁が言い渡した有罪判決が確定しているため、地検は再審請求を検討している。この事故は、04年6月16日に福岡市東区の交差点でトラックとバイクが衝突したもの。裁判ではトラック運転手が業務上過失傷害罪などに問われ、交差点でのバイクの停止位置が争点となった。調べによると、バイクに乗っていた伊藤容疑者は、知人を通じて知り合った長谷部容疑者に対し、自分が有利になるよううその証言を依頼。05年6月の公判で長谷部容疑者は、事故現場にいなかったにもかかわらず、伊藤容疑者の主張に沿った証言をした疑い。

同11月、福岡地裁はトラック運転手に懲役8カ月執行猶予4年の有罪判決を言い渡した。トラック運転手の上司が裁判の傍聴で疑問を感じ、長谷部容疑者を問いただしたところ、偽証を認めたため、今年2月に地検に告発した。

## Arrest of Drivers who made false statement in Court, Fukuoka Public Prosecutor's Office.

The Special Criminal Affairs Division of the Fukuoka Public Prosecutor's Office announced on the 7th that the arrest had taken place of Fukuoka Prefecture company workers Koiji Ito (35) of Minato in Shingo, and Katsutoshi Hasebe (34) of Uchihashi in Kasuya on suspicion of perjury. They are believed to have made false testimonies at a Public hearing in relation to a traffic accident. Because a guilty verdict was reached at Fukuoka district court on the basis of perjury, the Public Prosecutor is considering demanding a re-trial.

The accident took place on the 16th June 2004, when a truck and a motorbike collided on a crossroads in Higashiku, Fukuoka Prefecture. At the hearing, the driver was accused of causing injury through professional negligence, with the stopping point of the motorbike on the roundabout being the point at issue. According to the investigation, Ito had been riding on the motorbike, and he had requested Hasebe to make a false statement more advantageous to him. Ito had got to know him through an acquaintance. In June 2005 Hasebe testified in court according to Ito's request, regardless of the fact that he was not at the scene of the accident.

In November of that year at Fukuoka district court a prison sentence of 8 months with 4 years suspended was handed out to the lorry driver. The truck driver's boss had harboured doubts about what he had heard in court. After being questioned, Hasebe had admitted perjury, and in February of this year the truck driver's boss filed a complaint at the Public Prosecutor's Office.

| 英語 | 漢字 | ひらがな |
|---|---|---|
| District Public Prosecution | 地検 | ちけん |
| Perjury | 偽証 | ぎしょう |
| Collision | 衝突 | しょうとつ |
| Penal servitude | 懲役 | ちょうえき |

## Article 18
# Arrest of ¥19m Robber Suspects

2006年08月22日23時39分

1900万円強奪容疑で再逮捕女子大生誘拐2被告ら

千葉県船橋市の「サッポロビール千葉ビール園」駐車場で現金輸送車から約1900万円が強奪された事件で、県警は22日午後、住所不定、元山口組系暴力団関係者伊藤金男容疑者(49)ら広域強盗団のメンバー4人を強盗致傷容疑で再逮捕するとともに、指示役とされる岩手県矢巾(やはば)町、山口組系暴力団員青木学容疑者(41)も銃刀法違反(譲渡)の疑いで逮捕した。拳銃入手をめぐるトラブルから、青木容疑者が4人に襲撃を強要したと県警はみている。青木容疑者は容疑を否認しているという。他に強盗致傷容疑で逮捕されたのは、中国籍の無職李勇(29)と流山市南流山7丁目、無職湯浅恭市(56)と妻由美子(56)の3容疑者。調べでは、4人は2月3日正午ごろ、同ビール園駐車場で集金中の警備員をナイフで刺したり拳銃を突きつけたりするなどし、現金輸送車から現金を強奪した疑い。青木容疑者は4人に拳銃と実弾十数発を渡した疑い。

Re-arrest of suspects in robbery of 19M yen, two defendants implicated in kidnap of girl student.

Developments in the affair where around 19M yen was robbed from a cash transportation vehicle in the car park of the 'Sapporo Beer Chiba Beer Garden' in Funabashi, Chiba Prefecture. On the afternoon of the 22nd, the Prefectural police have re-arrested four members of the widely active gang of robbers headed by Akio Ito (49). It was formerly linked to the Yamaguchigumi crime syndicate, and is of unknown address. The four are charged with robbery with violence. Additionally, the police have also arrested Manabu Aoki (41), a member of the Yamaguchigumi crime syndicate, on suspicion of infringing the laws relating to guns and swords. He is from Yahaba in Iwate prefecture, from where he has had a role in directing events.

Because of problems to do with getting hold of a gun, the Prefectural police think that the suspect Aoki forced the four people to go on the raid. It is believed that Aoki denies any involvement. Others arrested on suspicion of robbery with violence are Chinese national Yong Li (29), unemployed, Kyoichi Yuasa (56) also unemployed, and his wife Yumiko (56) living in 7 Chome, Minaminagareyama, in Nagareyama City.

According to the investigation, around midday on the 3rd February, a guard who was collecting money in the car park of the beer garden was threatened with a pistol and stabbed with a knife by the four accused. It is thought that they then stole the cash from the money transportation vehicle. Aoki is accused of furnishing the four with the pistol and ten live rounds of ammunition.

| 英語 | 漢字 | ひらがな |
|---|---|---|
| Wide-ranging | 広域 | こういき |
| Fatal injury | 致命傷 | ちめいしょう |
| Assignment | 譲渡 | じょうと |
| Pistol | 拳銃 | けんじゅう |
| Extortion | 強要 | きょうよう |
| Attack, raid | 襲撃 | しょうげき |
| Live bullets | 実弾 | じつだん |
| Former | 元 | もと |
| Guard | 警備員 | けいびいん |

## Article 19
# Drunken Assault on Train

2006年08月25日16時00分

京都市職員が酔って電車で暴行、携帯壊す容疑で逮捕

JR琵琶湖線の車内で酔って暴れたとして、滋賀県警大津署は25日、京都市南部土木事務所職員、木下悟容疑者(56)滋賀県草津市木川町を暴行と器物損壊の疑いで逮捕した。調べでは、木下容疑者は24日午後9時10分ごろ、大津市内を走行中の新快速電車(姫路発米原行き)内で、携帯電話でメールをしていた男性会社員(47)に「何してるんや」と怒鳴りつけて胸ぐらをつかみ、男性の携帯電話を二つ折りにして壊した疑い。男性が二つ持っていた別の携帯で車内から110番通報し、木下容疑者を石山駅で降ろした。木下容疑者は帰宅途中で、かなり酔っていたという。

Kyoto city worker in drunken assault on train, breaks mobile phone arrested on suspicion.

Following an incident of drunken disorder on a train on the JR Biwako line, on the 25th officers from Otsu police station in Shiga Prefecture arrested a suspect for assault and damage to property. He is Satoru Kinoshita (56), a worker in the Public Works Dept. in the southern part of Kyoto, who lives in Kinokawa in Kusatsu City, Shiga.

According to the investigation, the suspect Kinoshita was in the fast commuter train travelling in Otsu City (from Himeji towards Maibara) at around 9.10 on the evening of the 24th. He grabbed hold of the lapels of a fourty seven year old male office worker who was texting on his mobile phone, and demanded to know what he was doing, before breaking the phone in two pieces.

The office worker called for help by ringing 110 from another mobile phone which he was carrying, and Kinoshita got off the train at Ishiyama station. Kinoshita was believed to have been in quite a drunken state while on his way home.

| 英語 | 漢字 | ひらがな |
|---|---|---|
| Assault | 暴行 | ぼうこう |
| Get drunk, to | 酔う | よう |
| Break down, to | 壊す | こわす |
| Shout, yell, to | 怒鳴る | どなる |
| Grab hold of, to | 掴む | つかむ |
| Lapels | 胸倉 | むなぐら |

# Article 20
# Fatal Stabbing of Man in Aichi-Anjo

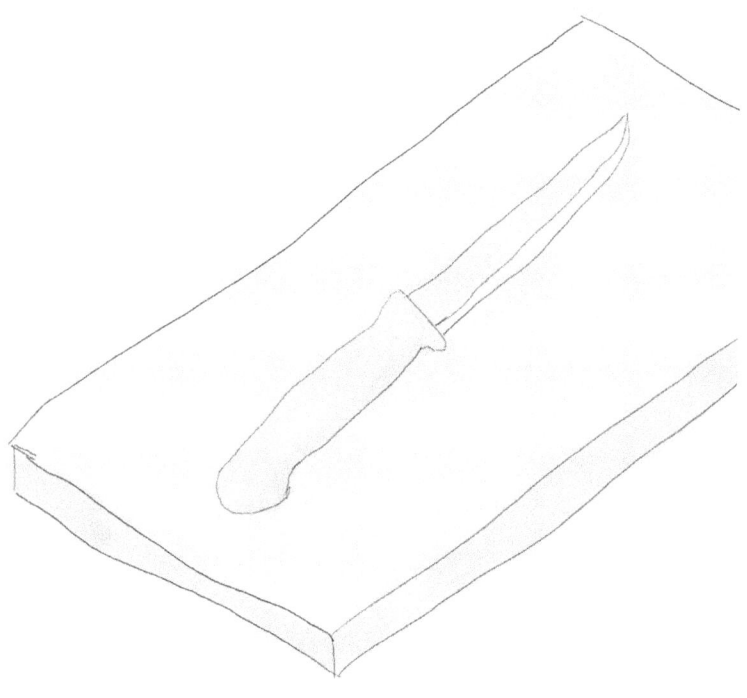

2006年08月25日16時00分

46歳男性が胸刺され死亡愛知・安城

26日午前7時40分ごろ、愛知県安城市赤松町、無職山本一夫さん(73)方から、「人を刺した」と119番通報があった。救急隊員が駆けつけたところ、山本さんの息子で同居している会社員の俊彦さん(46)が2階の居間で胸を刺されて倒れていた。俊彦さんは病院に運ばれたが、約1時間後に死亡が確認された。安城署は、包丁のような刃物を持っていた俊彦さんの妻(４２)が「自分が刺した」と認めたため、殺人の疑いで事情を聴いている。

Fourty-six year old man dies after being stabbed in chest Aichi-Anjo
============================================================

On the morning of the 26th at around 7.40, a 119 call announcing that a person had been stabbed was received from retired 73 year old Kazuo Yamamoto, of Akamatsucho in Anjo City, Aichi Prefecture. As an ambulance team rushed to assist, Mr. Yamamoto's son, company worker Toshihiko Yamamoto(46), collapsed after being stabbed in the chest in the second-floor living room of the flat which he shared with his father.

Toshihiko was taken to hospital, but his death was confirmed one hour later. Because Toshihiko's wife was in possession of a bladed tool similar to a kitchen knife, and because she admitted that she had herself carried out the stabbing, Anjo police are regarding her as a murder suspect.

| 英語 | 漢字 | ひらがな |
|---|---|---|
| First aid | 救急 | きゅうきゅう |
| Group member | 隊員 | たいいん |
| Chest | 胸 | むね |
| Inquire about, to | 聴く | きく |

Article 21

# Man Not Guilty of Professional Negligence

2006年08月21日15時38分

交通事故で業過致死に問われた男性に無罪札幌地裁

札幌市北区の市道を03年7月、自転車で横断中だった市立新川中学校3年生の長谷部拓磨君(当時14)を乗用車ではね死なせたとして、業務上過失致死罪に問われた同区の男性会社員(33)に対する判決公判が21日、札幌地裁であった。川田宏一裁判官は「過失を認めることはできない」などとして無罪(求刑禁固2年)を言い渡した。この事故は、道警の札幌北署が業務上過失致死容疑で男性を書類送検。その後、長谷部君の母親などが男性の過失を主張。地検は、発生から約3年たった今年3月に在宅起訴していた。判決では、男性が長谷部君を見てからブレーキをかけても間に合わず、衝突を回避することは難しかった、などとした。長谷部君が飛び出した可能性については言及しなかった。札幌地検の石田一宏次席検事は「判決は意外なもの。内容を検討し、対応したい」との談話を出した。

## Man accused of professional negligence death in traffic accident not guilty Sapporo court.

The court hearing and verdict on the male company employee (33) accused of causing death by professional negligence took place in Sapporo district court on the 21st. He was said to have caused the death while driving his car of Takuma Hasebe (14) a student at Shinkawa municipal middle school, who in July 03 was crossing a city road on his bicycle in the northern ward of Sapporo.

The judge Koichi Kawada handed out a not guilty verdict (the prosecution sought two years imprisonment) saying that he was not able to accept there had been blame.

In regard to the accident, the Hokkaido Prefectural police in the northern ward of Sapporo had sent a report to the prosecutor, with the driver accused of causing death by professional negligence. Afterwards, Hasebe's mother and others had insisted there had been a fault on the part of the driver. The district prosecutor's office had brought charges in March of this year, around 3 years after the incident had taken place.

The judgment stated that the man had braked after seeing Hasebe, but with insufficient space, it had been difficult to avoid a collision. There was no reference made to the possibility that Hasebe had suddenly appeared from nowhere. Sapporo District Court Assistant prosecutor Kazuhiro Ishida expressed surprise at the judgment, and announced that after consideration of the contents, he hoped to give a response.

| 英語 | 漢字 | ひらがな |
|---|---|---|
| Professional negligence | 業務上過失 | ぎょうむじょうかしつ |
| Lethal | 致死 | ちし |
| Error, blunder | 過失 | かしつ |
| Imprisonment | 禁固 | きんこ |
| Sending documents to a prosecutor | 書類送検 | しょるいそうけん |
| Collision | 衝突 | しょうとつ |

## Article 22
# Discovery of Murder Suspect's Body

2006年09月07日18時21分

容疑の男子学生、遺体で発見 徳山高専事件

山口県周南市の徳山工業高等専門学校で土木建築工学科5年の中谷歩(あゆみ)さん(20)が殺害された事件で、県警は7日、殺人容疑で逮捕状を取っていた同市に住む同級生の男子学生(19)の遺体を山口県下松市内で見つけた。男子学生は事件直後から行方がわからなくなっていた。近くで学生が乗っていたバイクも見つかった。県警は自殺とみて詳しく調べている。容疑者が死亡したことで、殺害動機など事件の全容を解明するのは難しくなった。遺体が見つかった場所は、下松市内の山陽自動車道の下松サービスエリアから西へ2キロ付近の山中。幅約2.5メートルほどの山道にバイクが立った状態で止まっているのを警察官が7日昼前に見つけた。遺体はバイクから数十メートル離れたところにあったという。一部白骨化しており、首を・つった状態だった。下松市は男子学生の家がある周南市の隣。調べでは、男子学生は8月28日、同校の研究室で中谷さんの首を絞めて殺害した疑いが持たれている。県警が現場に残された毛髪などの遺留物を鑑定したところ、男子学生のDNA型と一致したため、翌29日に逮捕状を取って行方を捜していた。中谷さんは8月28日午前10時ごろに友人の女性と登校。後で待ち合わせる約束をしたが、校内で別の学生2人と話をしたのを最後に、午前10時半ごろから行方がわからなくなった。友人が午後1時ごろから職員らとともに校内を捜し、午後3時ごろ、施錠されていた研究室の鍵を開

けて中に入った職員が、床に倒れている遺体を見つけた。中谷さんと男子学生はいずれもこの研究室に所属。鍵は担当教員のほか研究室に所属する全学生が普段から持っていた。研究室内に物色されたような跡はなく、近くの会議室にいた複数の学生も叫び声や不審な物音などは聞いていなかった。当日は夏休み中だったが、9月上旬にテストを控えていることなどから多くの学生が登校していた。こうした状況から県警は、顔見知りに不意に襲われた疑いが強いと判断。事件直後から行方のわからなくなっている男子学生が浮上した。何らかの理由で中谷さんを逆恨みしたか、突発的なトラブルなどで殺意を抱いたとみているが、容疑者の供述は得られなくなった。

## Discovery of body of suspected male student, Tokuyama Technical College incident.

There has been a fresh development in the case of Ayumi Nakatani (20), the murdered civil engineering and architecture student at Tokuyama Industrial Technical college in Shunanshi, Yamaguchi Prefecture. On the 7th, the Prefectural police discovered a body in Kudamatsu City, also in Yamaguchi Prefecture. The body was that of a 19 year male fellow student, living in the same city, and for whom the police had an arrest warrant on suspicion of murder. The male student had disappeared immediately after the murder. A motorbike which the student had been riding was discovered close by.

The Prefectural police are carrying out a detailed investigation on the assumption of suicide. The death of the suspect has complicated the emergence of all aspects of this affair, such as the motive for the murder. The spot where the body was discovered was in the mountains, in a vicinity 2 km west of the Kudamatsu service area on the Sanyo highway in Kudamatsu. A policeman made the discovery just before noon on the 7th, with the bike in an upright position with the engine turned off on a 2.5 metre wide mountain road.

It is reported that the body was ten metres from the motorbike. Partial decomposition had taken place, and the body was hanging by the neck. Kudamatsu is next to Shunanshi, where the male student's home is located. According to the investigation, it is suspected that the male student strangled Miss Nakatani in the college laboratory on the 28th of August.

The Prefectural police had an analysis made of hair left behind at the scene, and because there was a match with the DNA of the male student, on the following day they started to search for him with an arrest warrant.

Miss Nakatani was at the college with a girlfriend at around 10 am on the morning of the 28th of August. She made an arrangement to meet with her later, but after speaking with two other students in the college, from around 10.30 a.m. her whereabouts were unknown. Her friends and college staff started looking for her on the school premises from around 1 p.m. At around 3 p.m. staff gained entry to the locked laboratory with a key, and her body was found collapsed on the floor.

Miss Nakatani and the male student were part of the same laboratory group. As well as the staff in charge, all students belonging to the laboratory group also had a key. There was no trace of anything being searched for in the laboratory, and the many students who were in the meeting room next door heard no strange sounds or yells. Although that day was in the midst of the summer holidays, many students were present because of a test expected to take place during early September. In these circumstances, the Prefectural police have a strong suspicion that she had been suddenly attacked by an acquaintance. The male student had emerged as a suspect when he had gone missing immediately after the incident.

Whatever the reason, police think that he must have harboured an intention to kill because of some sudden trouble or because of resentment against Miss Nakatani, but a statement can no longer be obtained from the suspect.

| 英語 | 漢字 | ひらがな |
|---|---|---|
| Technical College | 高等専門学校 | こうとうせんもんがっこう |
| Skeleton | 白骨 | はっこつ |
| Hang, to (by the neck) | 首を吊る | くびをつる |
| Judgement, expert opinion | 鑑定 | かんてい |
| Match | 一致 | いっち |

# Article 23
# Drunken Driving in Hagi City

2006年09月17日19時24分

酒気帯び運転であて逃げ容疑萩市職員を逮捕

山口県警萩署は17日、同県萩市椿、市職員本清(ほんせい)貴之容疑者(34)を道路交通法違反(酒気帯び運転)の疑いで現行犯逮捕した。市によると、本清容疑者は市職員労働組合委員長。調べでは、本清容疑者は17日午前1時ごろ、酒を飲んで乗用車を運転した疑い。萩市内のコンビニエンスストアの駐車場で、停車中の軽乗用車に接触し、そのまま逃げたのを目撃した軽乗用車の男性が約1.5キロ追いかけて停車させ、110番通報。同署員が飲酒検知をしたところ、酒気帯び運転が判明したという。本清容疑者は「16日夕から市内の飲食店で友人とビールや焼酎数杯を飲んだ。タクシーで帰宅後、車で外出した」と話しているという。

<u>Suspect runs off after driving under the influence of alcohol Arrest of Hagi City employee.</u>

Police from the Hagi station in Yamaguchi Prefecture have caught red-handed Takayuki Honsei (34), a city employee in the Tsubaki district of the city of Hagi. He is accused of violating the road traffic regulations by driving whilst under the influence of alcohol. According to sources in the city, he is chairman of the Trade Union committee for the City's employees.

According to the investigators, Honsei is suspected of having driven his car at one o'clock in the morning of the 17th after the consumption of alcohol. After Honsei had driven into a stationary small car in the parking lot of a convenience store in Hagi, the owner of the vehicle witnessed him getting away. The owner pursued him for 1.5 kilometres, brought the car to a stop, and then dialled 110. When the police breathalysed him, it was demonstrated that he had been driving under the influence of alcohol.

It is believed that Honsei said that he had been drinking volumes of beer and spirits in the city's bars on the evening of 16th with a girlfriend. After returning home by taxi, he went out in his car.

| 英語 | 漢字 | ひらがな |
|---|---|---|
| Detector | 検知器 | けんちき |
| Hagi-city | 萩 | はぎ |
| Driving under the influence | 酒気帯び運転 | しゅきおびうんてん |
| Trade union | 労働組合 | ろうどうくみあい |
| Establish, prove, to | 判明する | はんめいする |

# Article 24
# Missing Taxi Driver Assaulted?

2006年09月19日

前夜に暴行受ける?大阪の不明タクシー運転手

大阪府茨木市の川の土手に車内に血痕のある個人タクシーが放置され、運転手の前久保要さん(59)同府高槻市 津之江町が行方不明になった事件で、タクシーが見つかる前日の16日深夜から翌日未明にかけ、高槻市でタクシーが絡む暴行事件があったとの情報が19日までに、茨木署捜査本部に寄せられたことが分かった。前久保さんのタクシーと同じ緑色で、クラクションが鳴らされ言い争うような声が聞こえたという。捜査本部は、このトラブルに前久保さんが巻き込まれた可能性があるとみて、近隣住民への聞き込みなどを進めている。見つかったタクシーの車外からは血液反応が検出されなかったことも判明。料金メーターは作動しており、捜査本部は何者かが営業中の前久保さんを襲撃し、車外に連れ出した後にタクシーを移動させて放置した疑いがある とみている。調べでは、運転席の背もたれやドアの下、後部座席の床に血痕があった。後部座席のマットには相当量の血が染み込んでおり、前久保さんが横たわっていたとみられる。一方、雑草が生い茂っていた車の周囲には血液反応はなく、前久保さんは放置現場に到着する前に連れ出されたとみられる。現場まで運転した別人の衣服に血液が付着した可能性もあるという。前久保さんは16日午後11時前、JR高槻駅で客を乗せたのを同僚に目撃されたのを最後に足取りが分からなくなった。

## Was he assaulted the night before? Whereabouts unknown of Osaka taxi driver.

It is understood that information about events leading up to the 19th has been the gathered by the Ibaraki Criminal Investigation headquarters in the case of missing taxi driver Kaname Maekubo from Tsunoecho, Takatsuki City, in Osaka Prefecture. His bloodstained private taxi was left abandoned on the riverbank in Ibaraki City, Osaka.

Between the evening of the 16th, the day before the discovery of the taxi, and the dawn of the following day, there was a violent incident involving a taxi in Takatsuki City. There had been quarrelling and the sounding of a car horn involving a taxi of the same colour as that of Mr Maekubo. The Investigation headquarters think it possible that Mr Maekubo was involved in this trouble, and are pursuing their inquiries with people in the neighbourhood.

It has been confirmed that no traces of blood had been detected from the outside of the discovered taxi. The taxi fare meter was still functioning, and the headquarters police suspect that someone attacked Mr Maekubo while he was working. After taking him from the car, the taxi was moved and then abandoned. According to the investigation, there were bloodstains on the backrest of the driver's seat, under the door, and on the floor of the back seat compartment.

| 英語 | 漢字 | ひらがな |
|---|---|---|
| Blood stain | 血痕 | けっこん |
| Attack, charge, raid | 襲撃 | しゅうげき |
| Eyewitness | 目撃 | もくげき |
| Trace | 足取り | あしどり |
| Permeate, to | 染み込む | しみこむ |

A considerable amount of blood had permeated the mat of the back seats, and it seems that Mr Maekubo may have laid himself down there.

However, no bloodstains had been found in the vicinity of the car where weeds were growing, and it may be that Mr. Maekubo was removed before the car arrived at its final spot for abandonment.

It is likely that the other person who drove to the spot will have had bloodstains on his clothing. There has been no trace of Mr. Maekubo after his final sighting by a colleague as he gave a lift to a customer at Takatsuki JR station, before 11 p.m. on the evening of the 16th.

Article 25

# Man Fled After Injuring Seven in Crash

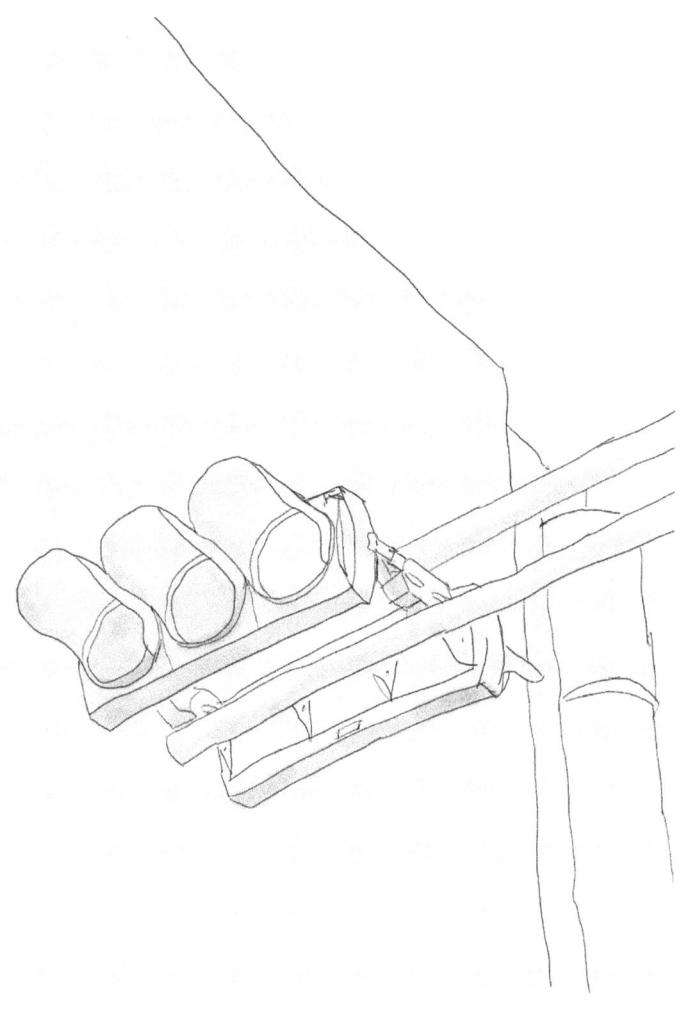

2006年09月19日

飲酒事故で4台に衝突、7人けがさせ逃走懲役3年の判決

飲酒後に乗用車を運転して車4台に衝突し、7人にけがをさせたなどとして、危険運転致傷と道路交通法違反(ひき逃げ)の両罪に問われた兵庫県尼崎市のとび職竹内光明被告(37)の判決が20日、大阪地裁であった。内田貴文裁判官は「飲酒によって正常ではない状態で運転し、信号無視を繰り返すなど無謀。同種事案が社会問題化しており、厳しい非難を免れない」として懲役3年(求刑懲役4年)を言い渡した。判決によると、竹内被告は1月30日午後10時半ごろ、大阪市淀川区の交差点で酒に酔って車を運転し、対向車4台に衝突して7人に重軽傷を負わせたまま逃走した。竹内被告は事故翌日の同31日に府警に出頭し、飲酒運転だったことを認めたが、府警は当時の飲酒量の特定が難しかったために業務上過失致傷とひき逃げの両容疑だけで逮捕、送検した。その後の大阪地検の補充捜査で、竹内被告が事故当日の夕方から焼酎やビールを飲んでいたことが分かり、同地検が法定刑がより重い危険運転致傷罪に切り替えて起訴した。

## Four cars hit in drunken crash, escaped after causing injury to seven people. Court hands out 3 year prison sentence.

After crashing into four cars while driving his own car in a drunken state and bringing about the injury of seven people, sentence was passed at Osaka district court on the 20th on defendant building worker Mitsuaki Takeuchi (37), of Amagasaki City in Hyogo Prefecture. He was accused both of infringing the road traffic laws (hit and run) and causing injury by dangerous driving. The judge Takafumi Uchida handed down a prison sentence of three years (the prosecution sought four years) explaining that Takeuchi had driven in an unfit condition due to alcohol and had been reckless in repeatedly ignoring traffic lights. This kind of case was becoming a social nuisance, and harsh censure could not be avoided.

According to the court summing-up, at around 10.30 p.m. in the evening of the 30th January, the defendant Takeuchi was driving his car while drinking alcohol at the Yodogawa crossroads in Osaka. He crashed into four cars coming in the opposite direction, causing both slight and serious injuries to seven people, and then took flight. The defendant Takeuchi appeared at the Prefectural police station on the 31st, the day after the accident, where he admitted he had driven under the influence of alcohol.

The Prefectural police could not at that point determine the exact amount of alcohol consumed, and having arrested him only on suspicion of professional negligence resulting in injury and hit-and-run driving, his case was referred to the Public Prosecutor's office.

Then the Osaka district prosecutor carried out a further investigation. Learning that Takeuchi had been drinking beer and

| 英語 | 漢字 | ひらがな |
|---|---|---|
| Hit-and-run | ひき逃け | ひきにげ |
| Case | 事案 | じあん |
| Get drunk, to | 酔う | よう |
| Spirits | 焼酎 | しょうちゅう |

spirits in the evening of the day of the accident, the prosecutor changed the charges to the more serious causing injury by dangerous driving.

## Article 26
# Fingerprint on Missing Taxi Drivers Door

2006年09月19日

天井灯から鮮明な指紋大阪・タクシー運転手不明

大阪府高槻市の個人タクシー運転手前久保要さん(59)が行方不明になっている事件で、同市南部の路上で発見されたタクシーの天井灯から前久保さんとは別人の鮮明な指紋が検出されたことが府警の調べで分かった。同市内の住宅団地で前久保さんとトラブルになっていた男がタクシーを運転して走り去る姿を住民が目撃しており、府警は男が逃走中に、天井灯を捨てた際に付着した可能性があるとみている。調べでは、指紋は、道路脇の自動販売機裏から見つかった天井灯から検出された。前久保さんや天井灯を拾った人、警察庁のデータベースとは一致しなかったという。指紋が鮮明であることから、前久保さんを襲った男の指紋の可能性があるという。同市南部の団地で、17日午前0時半過ぎ、前久保さんとトラブルがあったとみられる白いシャツ姿の男は、前久保さんのタクシーの運転席に乗り込み、急発進して団地の外に出たのを住民が目撃していたことも判明した。府警はこの男が前久保さんを襲った後、ほかの座席に移して運転していたとみている。

Clear fingerprint from roof light, unknown whereabouts of Osaka taxi driver.

In the case of the unknown whereabouts of private taxi driver Kaname Maekubo of Takatsuki, Osaka, it appears that the Prefectural police have found the distinct fingerprint of a person other than Maekubo on the taxi roof light discovered in a road in the city's Nanbu area. Residents in nearby residential apartment blocks witnessed the shape of a man involved in trouble with Maekubo driving off in the taxi. The Prefectural police think that it is likely that the mark was imprinted when the man threw away the roof light during his escape.

According to the investigators, the fingerprint was detected on the roof light which was discovered behind an automatic vending machine at the side of a road. There was no match on the metropolitan police database between the print of the man who had thrown the light away and the print of Maekubo. Because of the clarity of the fingerprint, it appears possible that it is the print of the man who attacked Maekubo.

It has become clear that after 12.30 a.m. in the morning of the 17th at the residential apartment block in the Nanbu area of the City, a resident witnessed a man in a white shirt who was in a dispute with Maekubo, who then climbed into the driving seat of his taxi, and made a rapid getaway from outside the block. The Prefectural police think that after he had attacked Maekubo, this man moved into the other seat and drove.

| 英語 | 漢字 | ひらがな |
|---|---|---|
| Roof light | 天井灯 | てんじょうとう |
| Fingerprint | 指紋 | しもん |
| Apartment block | 団地 | だんち |
| Run away, to | 走り去る | はしりさる |
| Stick to, to | 付着 | ふちゃく |
| Clear, distinct | 鮮明 | せんめい |

## Article 27
# Sewer Workers Killed by Toxic Fumes

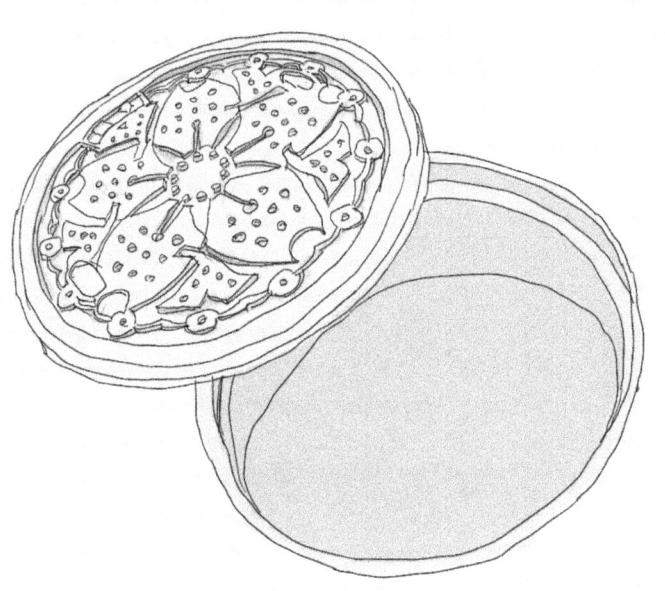

2006年09月19日

大阪・下水道作業員中毒死、市職員6人書類送検へ

大阪市港区で04年、マンホール内で下水道の点検作業をしていた市職員2人が硫化水素中毒で死亡した事故で、大阪府警は25日、同市都市環境局西部管理事務所の前副所長ら計6人を近く業務上過失致死容疑で書類送検する方針を決めた。事故死した管理主任(当時54)も現場責任者として容疑者死亡のまま送検する。府警は、前副所長らが作業前に硫化水素などの濃度を検査しなければ中毒事故が発生する可能性があると予測できる立場にありながら、検査をするよう指導しなかったと判断した。事故は04年8月、同区八幡屋1丁目の市道で、同事務所が道路陥没の原因調査で下水道管の亀裂の有無を点検していた際に発生。マンホール内(深さ約6メートル)に入った男性職員(当時30)と救助に入った管理主任が硫化水素中毒で死亡した。調べによると、職員らは直前まで、高圧洗浄機で下水道の汚泥を除去しており、汚泥がかくはんされたことで、下水道内の硫化水素濃度が急上昇し、酸素濃度が低下したとみられる。市のマニュアル「酸素欠乏危険作業保安管理要綱」は、マンホール内で作業する際、事前に硫化水素などのガス濃度を検知するよう規定していた。前副所長らは職員らに事前検査や呼吸器などの保護具を着用することを指導しなかった疑いが持たれている。府警は、前副所長ら幹部がマニュアルを守るよう職員に徹底せず、十分な安全対策を講じなかったと見ている。

Death by poisoning of men working in Osaka sewer, documents pertaining to six city employees sent to public prosecutor.

An accident took place in the Minato ward of Osaka in 2004, in which hydrogen sulphide poisoning killed two city employees who were carrying out sewer inspection work via a manhole. On the 25th the Osaka Prefectural police decided to forward to the Public Prosecutor documents accusing six employees of causing death by professional negligence. These six were close to the former deputy chief of the City's Environmental management office (western sector) of causing death by professional negligence. A management official who also died (at that time 54) will also be charged in relation to the deaths, since he was the person responsible at the actual scene.

The Prefectural police judged that the former deputy head and his team did not give management guidance on detection. This was in spite of being in a spot where the occurrence of accidental gassing could be expected, if monitoring of hydrogen sulphide was not carried out before work started.

The accident took place on a city street in Yahataya 1-chome in the Minato ward in August 2004. The people from this office were testing for the possible existence of a crack in a sewer pipe whilst looking for the cause of a road cave-in. A male worker (30) who had entered the manhole (around a depth of six meters) and a management official who had gone to rescue him were both killed by hydrogen sulphide poisoning.

According to the investigation, until just before the incident, the workers had been removing dirty mud from the sewer with a

| 英語 | 漢字 | ひらがな |
|---|---|---|
| Drain, sewer | 下水道 | げすいどう |
| Hydrogen sulphide | 硫化水素 | りゅうかすいそ |
| Concentration | 濃度 | のうと |
| Subsidence, cave-in | 陥没 | かんぼつ |
| Crack, crevice | 亀裂 | きれつ |
| Rescue, aid | 救助 | きゅうじょ |
| Dirty mud | 汚泥 | おでい |
| Oxygen | 酸素 | さんそ |
| Abide (by the rules) | 守る | まもる |

high-pressure cleaning machine. Because the dirty mud had been thoroughly stirred up, it seems that the concentration of hydrogen sulphide had rapidly risen, and the oxygen concentration had fallen.

The City manual entitled 'Principles of Safety Management in Operations with a risk of shortage of Oxygen' provides rules for the detection of concentrations of gases such as hydrogen sulphide before any work is carried out inside a manhole. It is suspected that the former deputy head and his team did not provide guidance either for the wearing of protective equipment such as breathing masks or for pre-work detection tests.

The Prefectural police consider that the boss and the former deputy chief and his team had not given adequate training in safety measures, and had not thoroughly coached the workmen to follow the manual.

## Article 28
# Fatal Hit and Run in Setagaya Ward

2006年09月19日

世田谷の死亡ひき逃げで運転手逮捕

今月6日、東京・世田谷区の路上でバイクに乗った男性がひき逃げされた事件で、警視庁はトラック運転手の男を逮捕しました。道路交通法違反などの疑いで逮捕されたのは、東京・武蔵村山市のトラック運転手、根本英二郎容疑者(44)です。調べによりますと、根本容疑者は今月6日、世田谷区大原の環状7号線でアル バイト、黒川翔太さん(23)がバイクで転倒したところをトラックではね、そのまま逃走した疑いが持たれています。黒川さんは出血性ショックでまもなく死亡しました。

警視庁はひき逃げ事件として捜査していましたが、現場周辺での聞き込みなどから根本容疑者のトラックが浮上、黒川さんの体に残されたタイヤの痕がトラックのタイヤと一致したことから逮捕したものです。

調べに対し根本容疑者は、「何かに乗り上げた 気がしたが、人かどうかはわからない」と容疑を否認しています。

Arrest of driver for fatal hit-and-run in Setagaya.

The metropolitan police have arrested a male truck driver in relation to the man riding his bike involved in the hit-and-run incident on a Setagaya road in Tokyo on the 6th of this month.

The man who has been arrested and accused of violating the road traffic laws is Eijiro Nemoto (44), a truck driver from Musashimurayamashi, Tokyo.

According to the investigation, on the 6th of this month Nemoto was suspected of fleeing the scene after his truck had run into part-time worker Shota Kurokawa, who had just fallen from his bike on the No. 7 Loop road at Oohara in Setagaya ward. Mr. Kurokawa suffered shock and loss of blood, and died soon after.

The metropolitan police carried out their investigations of the incident, treating the matter as a hit-and-run. Reports of Nemoto's truck emerged from inquiries made in the locality of the incident, and because traces of tyre remaining on Kurokawa's body matched the truck tyre, the police arrested him.

In his response to the investigators, the accused man Nemoto denied any wrongdoing, saying that he thought he had run over something, but didn't know whether it was a person or not.

| 英語 | 漢字 | ひらがな |
|---|---|---|
| Circle | 環状 | かんじょう |
| Tumble, fall off, to | 転倒する | てんとうする |
| Rise to the surface, to | 浮上 | ふじょう |
| Run aground, to | 乗り上げる | のりあげる |
| Hit, knock down, to | 撥ねる | はねる |
| Traces | 痕 | あと |

ARTICLE 29
# Image of Man in Gyudon Shop Robbery

2006年09月19日

牛丼店強盗事件で容疑者の似顔絵公開

今月、東京・豊島区の牛丼店に男が刃物を持って押し入り、現金13万円を奪って逃走した事件で、警視庁は容疑者の男の似顔絵を作成するとともに、防犯ビデオに映った男の姿を公開しました。

男は年齢30歳くらい、身長170センチほどで、黒の野球帽に黒いシャツ、黒いズボン姿です。今月17日午前5時半ごろ、豊島区西池袋の牛丼店にこの男が刃物を持って押し入り、現金およそ13万円を店員から脅し取りましたが、その3日後の今月20日、新宿区北新宿の牛丼店にも同一人物と見られる男が刃物を持って押し入り、現金およそ9万円を奪う事件が起きています。東京都内では、今月、牛丼店を狙った強盗事件がこのほかに2件相次いでいて、警視庁は関連を調べています。

Release to the public of likeness of suspect in gyudon shop robbery.

There has been a development in relation to the incident this month in Tokyo's Toshima ward when a man brandishing a bladed tool burst into the gyudon shop, and escaped after stealing 130,000 yen in cash.

The metropolitan police have drawn up a likeness of the male suspect, and have also released to the public the outline of a man captured on a security video. The man is about 30 years in age, around 170 centimeters tall, wearing a black baseball cap, black shirt and black trousers.

At around 5.30 a.m. in the morning of the 17th of this month, this man pushed his way into the gyudon shop in west Ikebukuro carrying a bladed tool, and took around 130,000 yen from the shop assistant whilst making threats. Three days after on the 20th in the gyudon shop in north Shinjuku in the Shinjuku ward, an incident occurred where once again someone who seemed to be the same man forced his way in whilst carrying a bladed tool and stole around 90,000 yen in cash.

This month in the Tokyo metropolitan area, two further robbery incidents targeting gyudon shops have taken place in succession, and the Metropolitan police are investigating links.

| 英語 | 漢字 | ひらがな |
|---|---|---|
| Rice covered with beef | 牛丼 | ぎゅうどん |
| Portrait, likeness | 似顔絵 | にがおえ |
| Baseball cap | 野球帽 | やきゅうぼう |
| Aim at, to | 狙う | ねらう |

# Vocabulary Lists

# Vocabulary lists

# English to Japanese

| 英語 | 漢字 | ひらがな |
|---|---|---|
| Abandonment | 遺棄 | いき |
| Abduction | 略取 | りゃくしゅ |
| Abide (by the rules) | 守る | まもる |
| Aim at, to | 狙う | ねらう |
| Alarm | 警報 | けいほう |
| Apartment block | 団地 | だんち |
| Appeal trial | 控訴審 | こうそしん |
| Appeal, to | 上告 | じょうこく |
| Arms, armament | 武装 | ぶそう |
| Arrest | 逮捕 | たいほ |
| Assault | 暴行 | ぼうこう |
| Assignment | 譲渡 | じょうと |
| Attack, raid | 襲撃 | しょうげき |
| Attempted murder | 殺人未遂 | さつじんみすい |
| Baseball cap | 野球帽 | やきゅうぼう |
| Bind tightly | 緊縛 | きんばく |
| Bind, to | 縛る | しばる |
| Blood stain | 血痕 | けっこん |
| Boss (Yakuza) | 組長 | くみちょう |
| Breach of trust | 背任罪 | はいにんざい |
| Break down, to | 壊す | こわす |

| 英語 | 漢字 | ひらがな |
|---|---|---|
| Burn, be roasted | 焼ける | やける |
| Bury, to | 埋める | うめる |
| Case | 事案 | じあん |
| Cause of death | 死因 | しいん |
| Cerebral contusion | 脳挫傷 | のうざしょう |
| Chest | 胸 | むね |
| Circle | 環状 | かんじょう |
| Clear, distinct | 鮮明 | せんめい |
| Collection, recovery | 回収 | かいしゅう |
| Collision | 衝突 | しょうとつ |
| Concentration | 濃度 | のうと |
| Confession | 供述 | きょうじゅつ |
| Confinement | 監禁 | かんきん |
| Corpse | 死体 | したい |
| Corpse, remains | 遺体 | いたい |
| Counterfeit money | 偽札 | にせさつ |
| Crack, crevice | 亀裂 | きれつ |
| Customs office | 関税局 | かんぜいきょく |
| Cut, to | 切る | きる |
| Death by suffocation | 窒息死 | ちっそくし |
| Defence counsel | 弁護団 | べんごだん |
| Defendant | 被告 | ひこく |
| Detector | 検知器 | けんちき |
| Die, to | 死ぬ | しぬ |
| Dirty mud | 汚泥 | おでい |

| 英語 | 漢字 | ひらがな |
| --- | --- | --- |
| Dishonesty | 不正 | ふせい |
| District public prosecution | 地検 | ちけん |
| Disturbance | 動揺 | どうよう |
| Drain, sewer | 下水道 | げすいどう |
| Driving under the influence | 酒気帯び運転 | しゅきおびうんてん |
| Duplicate key | 合鍵 | あいかぎ |
| Edged tool | 刃物 | はもの |
| Error, blunder | 過失 | かしつ |
| Escape | 逃走 | とうそう |
| Establish, prove, to | 判明する | はんめいする |
| Exposing | 摘発 | てきはつ |
| Extortion | 強要 | きょうよう |
| Eyewitness | 目撃 | もくげき |
| False | 偽 | ぎ |
| Faltering wound | ためらい傷 | ためらいきず |
| Family Court | 家裁 | かさい |
| Fatal injury | 致命傷 | ちめいしょう |
| Fingerprint | 指紋 | しもん |
| Fire | 火事 | かじ |
| First aid | 救急 | きゅうきゅう |
| Flight, desertion | 逃走 | とうそう |
| Followers (suffix) |  | ーら |
| Forced repatriation | 強制送還 | きょうせいそう |
| Forgery | 偽造 | ぎぞう |
| Former | 元 | もと |

| 英語 | 漢字 | ひらがな |
|---|---|---|
| Frame someone, to | 捏ち上げる | でちあげる |
| Fraud | 詐欺 | さぎ |
| Get drunk, to | 酔う | よう |
| Grab hold of, to | 掴む | つかむ |
| Group member | 隊員 | たいいん |
| Guard | 警備員 | けいびいん |
| Guilty | 有罪 | ゆうざい |
| Hagi (city) | 萩 | はぎ |
| Hang, to (by the neck) | 首を吊る | くびをつる |
| Hit and run | ひき逃げ | ひきにげ |
| Hit, knock down, to | 撥ねる | はねる |
| Hydrogen sulphide | 硫化水素 | りゅうかすいそ |
| Imprisonment | 収監 | しゅうかん |
| Imprisonment | 禁固 | きんこ |
| Inagawakai (gang) | 稲川会 | いながわかい |
| Infringement | 侵害 | しんがい |
| Inquire about, to | 聴く | きく |
| Investigation | 捜査 | そうさ |
| Investigation | 捜索 | そうさく |
| Investigation | 調べ | しらべ |
| Jail sentence | 実刑 | じっけい |
| Jewels | 宝石 | ほうせき |
| Judgement, expert opinion | 鑑定 | かんてい |
| Judicial decision | 判決 | はんけつ |
| Kidnapping | 誘拐 | ゆうかい |

| 英語 | 漢字 | ひらがな |
| --- | --- | --- |
| Killing | 殺害 | さつがい |
| Kitchen Knife | 包丁 | ほうちょう |
| Kosan Shinkin Bank | 興産信用金庫 | こうさんしんようきんこ |
| Lapels | 胸倉 | むなぐら |
| Leaving charge on file | 起訴猶予 | きそゆうよ |
| Legally ordered autopsy | 司法解剖 | しほうかいぼう |
| Length of a sword | 刃渡り | 刃渡り |
| Lethal | 致死 | ちし |
| Life sentence | 無期懲役 | むきちょうえき |
| Live bullets | 実弾 | じつだん |
| Loss, damage | 損害 | そんがい |
| Malpractice | 背任 | はいにん |
| Match | 一致 | いっち |
| Missing, be | 無くなる | なくなる |
| Missing, unaccounted for | 行方不明 | ゆくえふめい |
| Motive | 動機 | どうき |
| Murder | 殺人 | さつじん |
| Oxygen | 酸素 | さんそ |
| Patent rights | 特許権 | とっきょけん |
| Penal servitude | 服役 | ふくえき |
| Penal servitude | 懲役 | ちょうえき |
| Perjury | 偽証 | ぎしょう |
| Permeate, to | 染み込む | しみこむ |
| Pillage | 強奪 | ごうだつ |
| Pistol | 拳銃 | けんじゅう |

| 英語 | 漢字 | ひらがな |
|---|---|---|
| Police | 警 | けい |
| Police headquarters | 警視庁 | けいしちょう |
| Portrait, likeness | 似顔絵 | にがおえ |
| Presiding judge | 裁判長 | さいばんちょう |
| Principal Offender | 主犯格 | しゅはんかく |
| Proceeds | 売上金 | うりあげきん |
| Professional Negligence | 業務上過失 | ぎょうむじょうかしつ |
| Prohibition | 差し止め | さしとめ |
| Prosecution | 起訴 | きそ |
| Punishment | 受刑 | じゅけい |
| Raid, intrude, to | 侵入 | しんにゅう |
| Release, acquittal | 釈放 | しゃくほう |
| Rescue, aid | 救助 | きゅうじょ |
| Rice covered with beef | 牛丼 | ぎゅうどん |
| Rise to the surface, to | 浮上 | ふじょう |
| Rob, to | 奪う | うばう |
| Robbery | 強盗 | ごうとう |
| Roof light | 天井灯 | てんじょうとう |
| Run aground, to | 乗り上げる | のりあげる |
| Run away, to | 走り去る | はしりさる |
| Security company | 警備会社 | けいびがいしゃ |
| Self-protection | 護身 | ごしん |
| Sending documents to a prosecutor | 書類送検 | しょるいそうけん |
| Sentence (judicial) | 判決 | はんけつ |
| Shinkin Bank | 信用金庫 | しんようきんこ |

| 英語 | 漢字 | ひらがな |
|---|---|---|
| Shout, yell, to | 怒鳴る | どなる |
| Skeleton | 白骨 | はっこつ |
| Spirits | 焼酎 | しょうちゅう |
| Stab, to | 刺す | さす |
| Steal, to | 盗む | ぬすむ |
| Stick to, to | 付着 | ふちゃく |
| Strangle, to | 絞める | しめる |
| Strangulation | 絞殺 | こうさつ |
| Strike, to | 沈む | しずむ |
| Subsidence, cave-in | 陥没 | かんぼつ |
| Suicide | 自殺 | じさつ |
| Sumiyoshikai (gang) | 住吉会 | すみよしかい |
| Suspect | 容疑 | ようぎ |
| Taking captive | 拉致 | らち |
| Tear gas | 催涙ガス | さいるいガス |
| Technical College | 高等専門学校 | こうとうせんもんがっこう |
| Theft | 窃盗 | せっとう |
| Threaten | 脅迫 | きょうはく |
| Trace | 足取り | あしどり |
| Traces | 痕 | あと |
| Trade union | 労働組合 | ろうどうくみあい |
| Trial | 公判 | こうはん |
| Tumble, fall off, to | 転倒する | てんとうする |
| Under pretence | 装って | よそおって |
| Violation | 違反 | いはん |

| 英語 | 漢字 | ひらがな |
|---|---|---|
| Violent Gang | 暴力団 | ぼうりょくだん |
| Wages | 給料 | きゅうりょう |
| Wide-ranging | 広域 | こういき |
| Wield, brandish, to | 振り回 | ふりまわす |
| Wristwatch | 腕時計 | うでどけい |
| Yamaguchi-gumi (gang) | 山口組や | やまぐちぐみ |

# Vocabulary lists

# Japanese to English

| ひらがな | 漢字 | 英語 |
|---|---|---|
| あいかぎ | 合鍵 | Duplicate key |
| あしどり | 足取り | Trace |
| あと | 痕 | Traces |
| いき | 遺棄 | Abandonment |
| いたい | 遺体 | Corpse, remains |
| いっち | 一致 | Match |
| いながわかい | 稲川会 | Inagawakai (gang) |
| いはん | 違反 | Violation |
| うでどけい | 腕時計 | Wristwatch |
| うばう | 奪う | Rob, to |
| うめる | 埋める | Bury, to |
| うりあげきん | 売上金 | Proceeds |
| おでい | 汚泥 | Dirty mud |
| かいしゅう | 回収 | Collection, recovery |
| かさい | 家裁 | Family Court |
| かじ | 火事 | Fire |
| かしつ | 過失 | Error, blunder |
| かんきん | 監禁 | Confinement |
| かんじょう | 環状 | Circle |
| かんぜいきょく | 関税局 | Customs office |
| かんてい | 鑑定 | Judgement, expert opinion |

| ひらがな | 漢字 | 英語 |
|---|---|---|
| かんぼつ | 陥没 | Subsidence, cave-in |
| ぎ | 偽 | False |
| きく | 聴く | Inquire about, to |
| ぎしょう | 偽証 | Perjury |
| きそ | 起訴 | Prosecution |
| ぎぞう | 偽造 | Forgery |
| きそゆうよ | 起訴猶予 | Leaving charge on file |
| きゅうきゅう | 救急 | First aid |
| きゅうじょ | 救助 | Rescue, aid |
| ぎゅうどん | 牛丼 | Rice covered with beef |
| きゅうりょう | 給料 | Wages |
| きょうじゅつ | 供述 | Confession |
| きょうせいそう | 強制送還 | Forced repatriation |
| きょうはく | 脅迫 | Threaten |
| ぎょうむじょうかしつ | 業務上過失 | Professional Negligence |
| きょうよう | 強要 | Extortion |
| きる | 切る | Cut, to |
| きれつ | 亀裂 | Crack, crevice |
| きんこ | 禁固 | Imprisonment |
| きんばく | 緊縛 | Bind tightly |
| くびをつる | 首を吊る | Hang, to (by the neck) |
| くみちょう | 組長 | Boss (Yakuza) |
| けい | 警 | Police |
| けいしちょう | 警視庁 | Police headquarters |
| けいびいん | 警備員 | Guard |

| ひらがな | 漢字 | 英語 |
|---|---|---|
| けいびがいしゃ | 警備会社 | Security company |
| けいほう | 警報 | Alarm |
| げすいどう | 下水道 | Drain, sewer |
| けっこん | 血痕 | Blood stain |
| けんじゅう | 拳銃 | Pistol |
| けんちき | 検知器 | Detector |
| こういき | 広域 | Wide-ranging |
| こうさつ | 絞殺 | Strangulation |
| こうさんしんようきんこ | 興産信用金庫 | Kosan Shinkin Bank |
| こうそしん | 控訴審 | Appeal trial |
| ごうだつ | 強奪 | Pillage |
| ごうとう | 強盗 | Robbery |
| じょうと | 譲渡 | Assignment |
| しょうとつ | 衝突 | Collision |
| しょるいそうけん | 書類送検 | Sending documents to a prosecutor |
| しらべ | 調べ | Investigation |
| しんがい | 侵害 | Infringement |
| しんにゅう | 侵入 | Raid, intrude, to |
| しんようきんこ | 信用金庫 | Shinkin Bank |
| すみよしかい | 住吉会 | Sumiyoshikai (gang) |
| せっとう | 窃盗 | Theft |
| せんめい | 鮮明 | Clear, distinct |
| そうさ | 捜査 | Investigation |
| そうさく | 捜索 | Investigation |
| そんがい | 損害 | Loss, damage |

| ひらがな | 漢字 | 英語 |
|---|---|---|
| たいいん | 隊員 | Group member |
| たいほ | 逮捕 | Arrest |
| ためらいきず | ためらい傷 | Faltering wound |
| だんち | 団地 | Apartment block |
| ちけん | 地検 | District public prosecution |
| ちし | 致死 | Lethal |
| ちっそくし | 窒息死 | Death by suffocation |
| ちめいしょう | 致命傷 | Fatal injury |
| ちょうえき | 懲役 | Penal servitude |
| つかむ | 掴む | Grab hold of, to |
| てきはつ | 摘発 | Exposing |
| でちあげる | 捏ち上げる | Frame someone, to |
| てんじょうとう | 天井灯 | Roof light |
| てんとうする | 転倒する | Tumble, fall off, to |
| どうき | 動機 | Motive |
| とうそう | 逃走 | Escape |
| とうそう | 逃走 | Flight, desertion |
| どうよう | 動揺 | Disturbance |
| とっきょけん | 特許権 | Patent rights |
| どなる | 怒鳴る | Shout, yell, to |
| なくなる | 無くなる | Missing, be |
| もくげき | 目撃 | Eyewitness |
| もと | 元 | Former |
| やきゅうぼう | 野球帽 | Baseball cap |
| やける | 焼ける | Burn, be roasted |

| ひらがな | 漢字 | 英語 |
|---|---|---|
| やまぐちぐみ | 山口組 | Yamaguchi-gumi |
| ゆうかい | 誘拐 | Kidnapping |
| ゆうざい | 有罪 | Guilty |
| ゆくえふめい | 行方不明 | Missing, unaccounted for |
| よう | 酔う | Get drunk, to |
| ようぎ | 容疑 | Suspect |
| よそおって | 装って | Under pretence |
| らち | 拉致 | Taking captive |
| りゃくしゅ | 略取 | Abduction |
| りゅうかすいそ | 硫化水素 | Hydrogen sulphide |
| ろうどうくみあい | 労働組合 | Trade union |
| 刃渡り | 刃渡り | Length of a sword |
| ―ら |  | Followers (suffix) |

# Afterword

I hope that you found this book useful to your communicating with Japanese businesses.

If you have any suggestions, questions or feedback please do not hesitate to email me at stephen@specialist-trading.co.uk - I read and reply to all the emails I receive (English or Japanese is fine).

In addition, if you have a few moments to leave a review on the Amazon product page, please do.

I wish you every success with your study of Japanese & your business experiences. All the best & thank you for reading How to Write Japanese Business Emails.

Stephen

www.ingramcontent.com/pod-product-compliance
Lightning Source LLC
Chambersburg PA
CBHW050123020526
44112CB00035B/2361